ENLIGHTENED ENTREPRENEURSHIP

ENLIGHTENED ENTREPRENEURSHIP

How to start and scale your business without losing your sanity

CHRISTOPHER MYERS

ISBN-13: 9780692750018
ISBN-10: 0692750010

DEDICATION

To my wife, Nicki, who has put up with me through this crazy journey.

CONTENTS

FOREWORD

The mind is everything. What you think you become.

—BUDDHA

So what exactly is "Enlightened Entrepreneurship"? For me, it's a mindset that bridges the gap between your work and your life's work. It is a way of thinking that allows you to start and scale your company while retaining both your sanity and your soul.

I was just twenty-four years old when I started my company, BodeTree. Although I was blessed with a strong support network, the truth is that I had no idea what I was doing. All I knew is that I wanted to build something that helped people and created value—and that I wanted to do so without selling my soul.

I've made my fair share of mistakes throughout the course of my entrepreneurial journey, and I'm sure I'll make more before I'm done. These mistakes, however, have taught me more than any MBA class ever could. *Enlightened Entrepreneurship* was born from this iterative process of making mistakes and moving forward.

At the core, the philosophy is all about balance: finding balance between profits and people and between ambition and humility. Very few things in the world are as cut and dried as we humans would like them to be. Entrepreneurship is no different.

One thing I've come to realize is that everything, good or bad, starts in the mind. What you think is, in fact, what you become. If you focus on balance, self-awareness, and humility, those traits will become part of how you run your business.

It has been said that although there are no easy answers, there are simple answers. My goal in writing this book is to present simple solutions that can help fellow entrepreneurs find success doing the things they love.

Part 1: Starting Your Business

Few things in life are as exciting or terrifying as starting your own business. The seeds of success are planted long before the company is formed, and the journey toward gaining market acceptance is anything but easy. In this section, I explore five key areas:

- how to prepare for the entrepreneurial journey;
- how to structure your company;
- how to develop your product;
- how to get noticed; and
- how to gain traction.

BEFORE YOU START

MAKE YOURSELF INDISPENSABLE

Think back to all the teams you've worked with throughout your career. Chances are that there are a few individuals who stand out in your memory—individuals who were simply indispensable to the team and to the organization at large.

In today's work environment, the truly indispensable employee is becoming increasingly rare. Skills, knowledge, and relationships are more distributed than ever, across organizations of all sizes. When you couple this trend with the strong sense of entitlement that many modern employees show, it becomes easy to understand how team members can be seen as replaceable.

While there is certainly an element of responsibility on the part of the employer to create an environment where people can feel secure, I believe it is largely incumbent on employees to find ways to make themselves indispensable within their organization. I can speak with some degree of authority on this subject. I've gone through this process many times throughout my career as an employee, and now that I run my own company, my mission is to help my team members here at BodeTree do the same thing. When you're indispensable at work, you not only create your job security, but you also give yourself the opportunity to chart your course in life.

IDENTIFY YOUR STRENGTHS

First, you must possess the self-awareness to know your strengths and play to them accordingly. Too often, people try to force themselves down a path that is not right for their particular skills or interests. Early in my career, I fell victim to this behavior and tried to force myself down a path that simply wasn't right for me.

I began my career in consulting because I thought that was simply what one did after graduating from a business program. I focused on business valuation and financial reporting, diving headfirst into the world of financial modeling. It was a great learning experience, but I was never the best analyst at the firm. Technical finance wasn't something I naturally excelled at, and it certainly wasn't something I was passionate about.

I was always worried that I would be fired or surpassed by my more technically inclined peers. This led me to the realization that I wasn't playing to my strengths. I would never be the best analyst at the firm, and as a result, I would never be indispensable in that capacity.

I left that job and focused my efforts on more qualitative pursuits. I joined the strategy team of a Fortune 500 company and found my calling. I loved working with executives to bring a vision to life, and I was good at it. By playing to my strengths rather than trying to force myself into a role that wasn't right for me, I took the first step toward becoming an indispensable employee.

DEVELOP COMPLEMENTARY SKILLS

Once you identify your strengths, the next step is to develop skills that complement those strengths and that help you extract the most value from them. Too often, employees focus far too narrowly on the skills that are core to their position. For example, software developers tend to spend the bulk of their time learning new techniques and programming languages rather than developing the skills that help them communicate effectively and manage internal constituents.

While working on the strategy team at my former firm, I found that thinking through complex opportunities and various strategies came easily. However, I realized that if I couldn't get executives to buy into the vision, nothing would come of my hard work. I had to develop better communication skills in order to be an effective member of the team. It was at that point when I realized that employees become indispensable when they focus on their natural talents *and* master the skills that help them make the most of their strengths.

WORK HARDER THAN EVERYONE ELSE

Perhaps the most important step employees can take toward becoming indispensable is to outwork those around them. It sounds obvious, but when employees take ownership of tasks and put forth their full effort, members of leadership take note. Indispensable employees don't have to be asked to work late or come in early. They simply do what needs to be done to drive their projects toward success.

To my mind, attitude and behavior matter far more than natural ability. I'd rather have an earnest, hard-working employee who can take owner-ship of things and communicate with the team than someone who is just naturally brilliant. This hard work, coupled with the ability to recognize one's strengths and the drive to develop complementary skills, makes for an employee who is central to the operations of the company. These people have not only long-term job security but also the ability to chart their own course.

RECOGNIZE THE ACCELERATORS

Throughout my career, I've been fortunate enough to have great mentors who have been willing to take a chance on me and provide me with meaningful opportunities for growth. These mentors have not only taught me about what is important (both personally and professionally) but also given me several big breaks.

The value of the mentor-mentee relationship continues to be made clear to me each day. I know that I wouldn't be in the position I am in today if it weren't for the influence and guidance of my mentors. Here are the top three lessons I've learned about mentorship that I think can help anyone find career success.

DON'T BE AFRAID TO SEEK OUT MENTORSHIP

As the leader of a growing company, one thing that has always amazed me is the lack of enthusiasm that young employees tend to have about the concept of mentorship. I'm not sure whether it's simply a trait of millennials or something else, but I've never once had a team member actively seek out formal mentorship from senior members of the team.

If I could give young professionals one piece of advice, it would be to ask someone to mentor them. Mentors aren't going to go out of their way to drag someone along if that person doesn't show initiative. Mentorship is something that requires strong commitment from both parties, and it takes a lot of effort. The end results, however, are well worth it. I can personally attest that the lessons, connections, and opportunities that mentors provide are invaluable. It's up to you, however, to ask what mentors can offer—and to take advantage of it.

LEARN TO RECOGNIZE THE ACCELERATORS IN YOUR LIFE

My first job right out of college was an internship at a real-estate investment trust by the name of Cole Capital. It was an interesting place to work, but my role was of no particular importance. Still, I was thrilled to have the opportunity, and I put an insane amount of effort into even the most menial of tasks. This behavior caught the attention of the CEO's personal assistant, who went out of her way to connect me with him. This was a huge opportunity—but one that could have easily been overlooked.

Fortunately, I recognized the favor she was doing for me, and I ended up developing a very close relationship with the CEO, Christopher Cole. Mr. Cole was the first major accelerator in my career, and he quickly introduced me to the world of entrepreneurship, writing, and executive management. His influence on the trajectory of my life cannot be overstated, and I owe him a great debt of gratitude to this day.

REMEMBER THAT MENTORSHIP IS A TWO-WAY STREET

Too many young professionals fail to realize that mentorship is a two-way street. You have to deliver tremendous value to your mentor as well, and that often means working longer and harder than those around you work.

This lesson came into play with the second major accelerator and mentor in my life—my cofounder at BodeTree, Matt Ankrum. Matt hired me to work on his strategy team at Apollo Group after an extensive search process. I really wanted the job, and I committed to outworking everyone so that I could get it. I went out of my way to develop a strong strategy proposal for the team, going so far as to have it professionally designed and printed. Although this might seem like a trivial thing, it helped me stand out among other candidates who were better qualified. It also proved to Matt that I was dedicated to delivering exceptional value to him and the rest of the team.

This attitude continued after I was hired, and I made a point of working harder and longer than anyone else worked in order to make the team more successful. Toward the end of our tenure at Apollo, Matt managed to coax the initial concept for BodeTree out of me. Much to my surprise, he not only supported the idea but also wanted to be part of it. He took a huge chance on his young employee because he believed in the vision and passion that I brought to the table. Had I failed to work hard for him and prove my dedication, BodeTree would never have been born. Nearly everything that has led me to this point in my life has been a direct result of my having worked to provide tremendous value to my mentors.

I firmly believe that—hands down—mentorship is the best path to career success. The benefits you can gain from a good mentor relationship can outweigh the benefits of attending grad school, natural ability, and even dumb luck. The key is to have the foresight and humility to ask to be mentored. If you start there, you'll find there are plenty of accelerators in your life who can add value. More important, you can take it on yourself to add tremendous value for them. In doing so, you'll ensure that you get the most out of the mentor relationship and find success in your life and career.

FIND YOUR FLOW

Nothing saddens me more than seeing people living their lives in quiet desperation, stuck in careers that are both uninspiring and unfulfilling. James Taylor once said, "You can play the game and act out the part, even though you know it wasn't written for you." In the world of business, this tragic situation occurs when an individual's natural skills and proclivities are simply not a fit for the career he or she chose. That's why I believe that finding the right fit, both in terms of natural skills and interest, is the most important factor when it comes to success.

When people find their fit, they experience a state of happiness and creativity called *flow*. Hungarian psychologist Mihaly Csikszentmihalyi popularized the concept of flow in the early 1990s. According to his theory, flow manifests itself when a person's natural skills align with the challenges he or she faces. Not surprisingly, when people operate outside their flow, problems arise. For example, if an individual works in a highly challenging environment in which his or her natural skills are outclassed, that person tends to experience terrible anxiety and stress. Conversely, if an individual's advanced skills are wasted in an industry that is neither interesting nor challenging, boredom and apathy quickly set in.

Finding your personal flow in the context of work isn't easy. Fortunately, there are a few key lessons I've learned over the years that can help you find your place in the workplace and avoid a life of quiet desperation.

BE HONEST ABOUT YOUR STRENGTHS AND WEAKNESSES

I began my career in consulting, because that's what young business school graduates do. I wanted to do something more creative and entrepreneurial, but I was afraid to take on the risk at the time. These were tough years for me, because no matter how hard I worked, it just didn't feel right. I tried hard to conform to the ideal of what a hotshot consultant should be even though I knew that wasn't who I was. As a result, I was constantly anxious about my performance relative to my peers', and I stressed out over everything.

It was only when I took the time to be honest about who I really was that things started to improve. I grew to understand that my natural strengths are at the intersection of finance and the humanities instead of in analytics. Once I began to see myself as someone with the soul of an artist trapped inside of a finance guy's body, things started to make sense. I realized that I'd never be successful or happy as a consultant and that my ideal state of flow would be found elsewhere. This sent me down the path of entrepreneurship and ultimately led to the founding of my company, BodeTree.

Don't Let Yourself Get Too Comfortable

The thing about financial consulting is that it generally pays pretty well. The personal comfort that came along with the job that I hated was the one thing that gave me pause when it came time to quit. I found that I could put up with a lot of short-term pain as long as I was well compensated. Of course, this was an utterly miserable way to live my life, but I'd be lying if I said that money wasn't a consideration. Ultimately, my desire to make a dent in the universe outweighed my desire for a comfortable lifestyle, but that isn't the case for everyone.

For too many, the allure of comfort and the fear of financial hardship prevent them from ever making a positive change. My advice is to avoid getting too comfortable in a career that you know isn't right for you. Once you pass the metaphorical point of no return, you've committed yourself to a path that is both stifling and unfulfilling.

Learn to Take Risks

I'll never forget the day I told my wife that I wanted to quit my well-paying job and start a company called BodeTree. She was months away from giving birth to our first child, and here I was—proposing to eliminate any semblance of stability we had in our lives. Still, despite the risks, we both knew it was the right thing to do, and she gave me her full support. I was lucky in that when the opportunity for me to find my flow presented itself, I had the ability and the support I needed to take advantage of it. Many people aren't able to make that sort of a jump, and thus they miss out when opportunities present themselves.

Life is messy, difficult, and complicated. Nothing ever comes easily, and timing is rarely on your side. If you find yourself waiting for the perfect time or circumstances to make a change, you'll never be able to move forward. You have to get comfortable taking risks both big and small if you want to find your perfect state of flow. This can be both scary and difficult, but risk and reward go hand in hand. Finding your personal flow is important for finding not only success in your career but also happiness and balance in life. Life is too short to live it in quiet desperation, so be honest with yourself, don't get too comfortable, and learn to take risks. You'll be happy that you did.

FORGET ABOUT WORK-LIFE BALANCE

A while back, I was invited to attend Arizona State University's Spirit of Enterprise awards. The program was designed to honor the most influential entrepreneurs who have come out of the W. P. Carey School of Business. My family and I were in Arizona for Thanksgiving around that time, so I decided to invite my wife along as well. Bill Lavidge, CEO of Lavidge, a Phoenix-based advertising agency, gave the keynote, in which he outlined the top ten business lessons he'd learned over his long career. Number ten was titled "Work-Life Balance," and when the slide came up, my wife gave me a nudge and a smile.

"Work-life balance is a joke!" exclaimed Lavidge, much to my wife's surprise and my pleasure. Bill went on to explain that the commonly held vision of work-life balance doesn't apply to successful entrepreneurs. I wholeheartedly agreed with Bill's comments. The idea of work-life balance is something that has weighed heavily on my mind over the past few years, ever since starting BodeTree back in 2010.

FOR ENTREPRENEURS, WORK IS LIFE, AND LIFE IS WORK

I honestly don't feel like I have a job in the traditional sense of the word. For me, jobs are things you do because you need money or some way to keep busy. You clock in and out, and maybe, if you're lucky, you learn a thing or two along the way. I do not have that kind of job. As the CEO of BodeTree, I get to do what I love every day. Never once have I dreaded going into the office or working with my team.

The old saying that you should "do what you love, and you'll never work another day again" isn't true. There is always work to be done. What is true, however, is that if you do what you love, it will never feel like a job. That's why the idea of finding work-life balance as an entrepreneur is a joke. Work and life sit together on a spectrum, and when you try to separate the two, you're courting disaster. In my mind, there is nothing more frustrating than an entrepreneur who doesn't live and breathe his or her business. Does that mean that you ignore your family and friends? Absolutely not. They're simply part of the entire experience.

EXCEPTIONAL RESULTS REQUIRE EXCEPTIONAL EFFORT

Building a business is one of the most difficult things anyone can do. You have to be all in, all the time. No one is going to build your business for you. Exceptional results require exceptional effort from everyone involved, especially the founders. To quote Bill Lavidge again, "If you're going to succeed, you're going to have to work your butt off." It takes a special type of person to look at this massive challenge and embrace it with open arms, but that's what separates entrepreneurs from the rest.

This is where things can get sticky, especially when you have a family. There are times when you have to sacrifice time with your loved ones for the sake of the business. If that seems like a bitter pill to swallow, that's because it is. It's simply a trade-off that you have to make at some point. When I was a child, my father traveled extensively and worked incredibly long hours. This meant that he occasionally missed out on family events such as school ceremonies. He also provided incredibly well for his family and friends. The hard work that he put in resulted in the success he was able to share with others. There was no shortcut, and it's the same for entrepreneurs today.

ENTREPRENEURSHIP IS A WAY OF LIFE, NOT A MATTER OF WORK

While the "dream" of work-life balance is essentially unattainable for entrepreneurs—as it is for many others who love their work—there are ways to blend business and family successfully. My wife and I have a young son and will likely have another child in the coming year. I strive to be a good father even though I work long hours. The key is to blend the two and foster respect for hard work among your family members. In fact, as I write this, my four-year-old son is snuggled next to me, pretending to type on his iPad. As my team can attest, my family members come into the office on a regular basis and are involved in a variety of ways. I don't have to worry about work-life balance, because it's all the same to me.

So yeah, work-life balance is a joke—at least for entrepreneurs. There's just life, and the business that you work so hard to create is a huge part of that. The entrepreneur's way of life is not for everyone; there are plenty of sacrifices you have to make along the way. However, if you recognize that exceptional results require exceptional work and foster a spirit of entrepreneurship among your family members, you'll find that it's worthwhile.

EVERY BUSINESS HAS A GOD PARTICLE

Physics speaks of a mysterious and elusive particle called the Higgs boson, commonly known as the God Particle. The God Particle is believed to be the thing that gives mass to matter, and it represents the most fundamental component of the universe. After reading about the God Particle, I couldn't help but think that the concept behind it applies to business as well. Every business ultimately boils down to a single belief that forms the foundation of everything it does. Finding your business's God Particle, however, can be as elusive as finding the real thing.

FINDING YOUR COMPANY'S GOD PARTICLE

Identifying what makes up the "mass" of your company can be a challenge and may take several iterations, but it's well worth it in the end. It all comes down to the core value that your company provides to the marketplace. Often it is a more abstract and generalized concept than you might think.

Take Google, for example. Historically, Google's mission has been "to organize the world's information and make it universally accessible and useful." When the company was originally founded as a search-engine provider, this definition must have seemed both broad and grandiose. However, it provided the foundation for the company's ultimate expansion into new markets and has guided all Google's decisions.

BodeTree's God Particle is the liberation of data through authentic human interaction. We believe that great things can be accomplished through data—but only if that data comes from genuine, simple, and authentic interactions with the small businesses we serve. Without those engagements and relationships—with partners and customers alike—BodeTree wouldn't be any different from other technology providers. Our interactions form the foundation for who we are and why we do what we do.

THERE'S NO "I" IN TEAM, BUT THERE IS A GOD PARTICLE

As with most business philosophies, the idea of a God Particle won't be productive in your business without the buy-in of your team members. Think of it as a rallying cry that influences every aspect of the business—from what you build, to who you hire, and with whom you choose to work. It's vitally important that there be an accurate and consistent understanding of just what your company's God Particle is and what it means for your products, team members, and customers.

A clear, concise, and well-communicated God Particle provides teams with a common perspective and context for communicating. It enables team members, regardless of position, to boil down their thoughts, ideas, and communication strategies to their simplest form and align them with the mission of the organization. It makes communication, execution, and ethics easier.

BE THE PERSON YOUR GOD PARTICLE THINKS YOU ARE

We've all seen the bumper sticker: "Be the person your dog thinks you are." The same goes for your God Particle. When your God Particle is baked into each decision you make, it will be easier to become the company you truly want to be—the one your customers deserve. As I've discussed before, authenticity is the most important virtue any business (or individual, for that matter) can demonstrate. Authentic brands like Apple Computer, Patagonia, and Whole Foods know precisely what their God Particles are and demonstrate it in everything they do.

Each time you're faced with a decision—hiring new employees, establishing new partnerships, leaving your office door open or closed—reflect briefly on your God Particle. Ask yourself, "Is this decision representative of what we're made of?" and let that answer guide your choices.

The "God Particle" nickname grew out of the long, drawn-out struggles of physicists to find this elusive piece of the cosmic puzzle. Its very existence is central to both our understanding of the universe and our place in it, yet it is largely undetectable and poorly understood. The same can be said for most businesses and their God Particles. It is far too easy for companies to become so caught up in the day-to-day drudgery of running a business that they forget why they exist in the first place. Identifying the beliefs and values that give mass to your actions is central to becoming an authentic organization. Take the time to reflect on what your God Particle is, and then challenge your team members to put it at the center of everything they do.

MAKE THE MOST OF OPPORTUNITIES

I'm sure of two things in this world. The first is that life is a journey, full of twists and turns. The second is that hardly anything goes according to plan. Life's unpredictability isn't necessarily a bad thing. Sometimes the most unexpected events can change your personal trajectory in fantastic ways.

Whether you're meeting your spouse or finding your calling, opportunities don't take your personal timeline into consideration. Instead, they present themselves at arbitrary and frequently inopportune times. If you're not careful, it can be easy to miss them altogether. The trick is to develop the skills and character traits that help you identify and take advantage of these accelerator opportunities when they pop up. Here are three lessons I've learned that have helped me make the most of opportunities that have come my way.

LESSON ONE: BREAK OUT OF YOUR COMFORT ZONE

Fear is the root of almost all missed opportunities. People have a tendency to grow comfortable with what is familiar and to overestimate potential negative effects of risk. I've found that it's important, both for personal and entrepreneurial development, to consistently push the boundaries of your comfort zone. My first lesson with this came when I was nineteen years old and just wrapping up my freshman year at college. My entire life up to that point had been comfortable and stable. My family was as close to the Norman Rockwell ideal as a life can be, and as a result, I found myself growing complacent. I knew that I wanted to live a more dynamic life in the future, and the complacency I saw taking hold shook me to my core.

I decided that the solution to this problem would be to travel abroad, and not just to a comfortable and well-known destination. After looking at all the options, I settled on Romania. After all, the rural villages of former Soviet republics were about as far removed from suburban Phoenix, Arizona, as I was going to get. I knew that this transition would be difficult, but the culture shock and (relative) adversities I encountered made me stronger. Throughout the experience, I gained confidence, encountered new and fascinating people, and banished the complacency that had previously shaken me. I learned that fortune does, in fact, favor the bold and that I would have to continue taking risks in order to live the life I wanted. For me, there are few tragedies greater than failing to live up to your potential. Breaking out of my comfort zone was vital to avoiding that failure.

Lesson Two: Find a Mentor

Throughout my career, I've been fortunate to have great mentors who were willing to take a bet on me. These mentors have not only taught me about what is important (both personally and professionally) but also given me several big breaks. It's easy to take a mentor for granted and let the relationship fall to the wayside. Too many young professionals fail to realize that mentorship is a two-way street.

Lesson Three: Remember That Character Is King

I have known my two best friends since I was eleven years old. We went through middle school, high school, and college together. I even worked with one of them for years later on in my career. They also happen to be geniuses (and identical twins, but that's beside the point).

This instilled in me a strong sense of competition and more than a little bit of insecurity as we constantly pushed one another to outperform. This competitive nature and sense of insecurity followed me to my career at Cole, and I felt that, in order to be successful, I had to be the smartest guy in the room. Unfortunately, I'm rarely the smartest guy in any room. I found that the only way I could compete was by working harder than everyone else, staying humble, and being the easiest person to work with.

When I started to find some success in the role, I was puzzled at first. After all, I hadn't come up with any brilliant ideas or solved any major problems on my own. Then Mr. Cole took me aside and told me that the reason he wanted to work with me was that I was hard-working and valued honesty and humility. I realized then that character—not simply raw ability—is what matters. If you focus on building personal relationships and demonstrating character, mentors and others will respond and will want to help accelerate your trajectory.

When I asked Matt, my cofounder, why he took such a risk with me, his answer was the same: he wanted to work with people he trusts, respects, and admires. While ability is always a factor, it isn't the most important trait that he looked for. For him, character was, and always will be, king.

I don't believe in luck. I also don't believe that people can bend the universe to their will. I think that luck is just a lazy term for being able to attract, identify, and take advantage of the opportunities that come your way. Achieving this is both incredibly simple and incredibly hard. I think of it as being a three-stage process.

First, you have to learn to be bold and break out of your comfort zone. People may think you're crazy, but opening yourself up to a broader world is the first step to finding new opportunities. Second, find a mentor, and then deliver exceptional value to him or her. If you work hard, stay humble, and are easy to work with, people will take notice and accelerate your career. Finally, don't get caught up in trying to be the smartest person in the room.

Ability is important, but character always wins out. People, especially the mentors who can change your life, want to surround themselves with people whom they trust, respect, and admire. I don't have a magic formula, but I do believe that these lessons will go a long way in helping you make the most of your opportunities and get the most out of the accelerators in your life.

BUILDING YOUR COMPANY

IF YOU DON'T HAVE COMPETITION, YOU HAVE A PROBLEM

Deep down, every entrepreneur fears competition. After all, building a business is a deeply personal endeavor, and the very thought of having someone else try to play in your sandbox can elicit feelings of anxiety and defensiveness. The absence of competition in any given market segment is often viewed as a positive by entrepreneurs, providing them with a clear and straightforward path to success.

This belief, however, is as damaging as it is misguided. Entrepreneurs who don't have competition should be wary. Rather than being a strength, a lack of competition in your market can be indicative of a serious weakness. I should know: my business lacked competition for years, and it was a major problem. Looking back, I'm embarrassed by how I gleefully proclaimed our lack of competition to potential partners and investors. What I didn't realize at the time was that there are only a handful of reasons why a business might not have competition, and none of them is good.

REASON ONE: YOU'RE BEING TOO NARROW

The first reason why a business might not experience competition is an overly narrow definition of the target market. When you're building a product, it can be easy to become so engrossed in the details that you lose sight of the big picture. Put another way, although there might not be another solution in the market that does exactly what you do, there may be other players who are close enough that your prospective clients can't tell the difference.

I fell victim to this myself during my first year in business. I saw BodeTree as such a unique and targeted product that I convinced myself that we had little to no competition. After all, no other player in the market did exactly the same thing we were doing. I had a very narrow view of what constituted competition, and so I failed to see the forest for the trees.

In reality, our potential customers weren't looking for specifically what we offered. Instead, they were looking for broad solutions that could address the pain that they were experiencing in their business. This meant that we were competing not only against other web applications but also against things as diverse as bookkeepers, accounting platforms, and spreadsheets.

It was only after we expanded our view of what constituted competition that we truly began to understand the market we served. This realization helped us better connect with our customers, refine our messaging, and explain why our solution was superior.

Reason Two: You're Ahead of the Market

The second reason why your business might not have any competition is that you're simply ahead of the market. Of all the reasons, this is by far the least problematic. After all, you could simply be solving a major pain point for your customers in a new and innovative way. However, if that is the case, you have to be aware of the challenges that go along with being an innovator.

Contrary to what we would like to believe, many of us don't embrace change with open arms. As a result, it can be difficult for innovative companies to thrive when carving out an entirely new segment. This was the second issue I encountered at BodeTree. When we first launched our BodeTree Platform product, aimed at banks and other financial institutions, we found that we were about eighteen months ahead of the market.

Many of the banks and other institutions we were trying to serve simply weren't prepared for our solution. BodeTree didn't fit into the standard set of solutions with which they were familiar, and thus the sales process was incredibly challenging.

To solve this, we embarked on a massive campaign to educate our clients about the problem we were solving. In time, the market began to recognize the need for our solution, and competition began to appear. We were able to use this educational period to establish ourselves as thought leaders early on, and we developed an "awareness advantage" that remains even though we now have increased competition.

REASON THREE: YOU DON'T HAVE A PRODUCT THAT PEOPLE WANT

The third and final reason for a lack of competition is the hardest for entrepreneurs to accept: people simply don't want your product. This difficult possibility is something that we all have to be open to, as painful as it may be.

Grappling with the possibility that people may not want your product or solution requires a healthy dose of humility and self-awareness. To create something from scratch, entrepreneurs have to be both intellectually and emotionally invested. However, this deep, personal investment can often blind people to the facts.

I'll be the first to admit that the first iteration of BodeTree wasn't a success. At the time, the market we served was so small that it was nearly impossible for us to gain critical mass. Fortunately, we recognized that the people we were selling to didn't want the product we were selling, and we were able to pivot quickly and successfully.

Make no mistake: a lack of competition for your product or service is a weakness, not a strength. It means that you're in for a tough start. The key is to remain open-minded, self-aware, and mindful of the challenges you're going to encounter. Remember that competition is validation for your product or service: it should be celebrated rather than dreaded.

STAY HUNGRY BUT COMFORTABLE

As with most things in life, managing compensation issues inside a start-up is all about balance. Whether determining your own salary or recruiting new hires, it's vitally important to get it right. Compensation is an issue that I've struggled with constantly since starting BodeTree nearly five years ago.

With each passing milestone, there are new variables to consider and business needs that must be met. Over time, I've identified three principles that have helped me navigate these issues and make decisions for our team.

Prior to starting my own business, I held a very comfortable position at a Fortune 500 company. When it came time to leave and focus exclusively on BodeTree, I had to make a decision about how much money to pay myself. That first year was stressful. Not only were we stretched thin because of long hours spent developing our product, but we were also often distracted from the tasks at hand because of money concerns.

Painful as they may have been, these struggles helped me form an overarching philosophy about compensation going forward. As the business grew and became more profitable, I was able to apply what I learned to my ever-expanding team.

The last thing you want, as a founder, is for people to be distracted by money worries. That's never a good thing when you're already asking people to pour their blood, sweat, and tears into the business. The trick is finding a balance that allows people to maintain a level of comfort that alleviates financial stress while still staying hungry and motivated. First, you have to be in line with industry compensation. Second, you have to make sure that the people you hire aren't interested in a cash grab. Your early hires have to buy fully into the mission and long-term opportunity.

NEVER UNDERESTIMATE THE VALUE OF NONCASH COMPENSATION

Working in a start-up has many benefits for ambitious employees. The dynamic, fast-paced environment that start-ups foster allows employees to learn more and progress faster than in traditional workplaces. When I hire new employees, especially young professionals, I always emphasize the value of the experience they'll gain. For example, a new hire without a ton of direct experience may have the opportunity to interact with executives at top national firms, savvy investors, and influential members of the media on a daily basis. Those opportunities simply don't exist at most traditional companies.

There's also the opportunity for equity-based compensation. While we are judicious in how we hand out stock options, we make sure that reasonable equity positions are part of every key employee's overall package. This ensures that everyone on our team is properly motivated for the long haul and has an authentic appreciation for the overall well-being of the company. Equity isn't an alternative to cash, but it is an important component of a well-rounded compensation strategy.

Don't Lose Sight of the Big Picture

The most important advice I can offer when it comes to determining compensation is never to lose sight of your goals. Many times founders will cut off their noses to spite their faces when it comes to dealing with compensation issues.

Consider a scenario in which one of your key team members asks you to increase his or her base salary beyond what is generally considered market value. Rather than immediately dismissing the idea, a smart founder will take the time to consider the big picture. If that team member has a strong relationship with a big potential client, it might make sense to break the "comfortable but hungry" rule in order to protect the larger strategic opportunity.

Compensation isn't simply about determining salaries. It's about nurturing your most important asset—your team. Everyone is different, but if you always put your people first and determine what motivates them, you can't go wrong. Founders should strive to strike the right balance between cash, opportunity, and equity while remaining mindful of the big picture.

STAND OUT FROM THE CROWD

I'll be the first to admit that my company's name is nontraditional, to say the least. The name BodeTree came from the story of the Bodhi Tree, under which the Buddha is said to have achieved total enlightenment. It's a little out there, especially for a fintech company. However, I've found that there is much to be said for having a nontraditional business name. As with everything, there are pros and cons, but a properly chosen nontraditional name can positively differentiate your business.

DARE TO BE DIFFERENT

Consider, for a moment, the naming of Kim Kardashian and Kanye West's son. For those of you who may not be aware, the child's name is Saint West. I don't think anyone expected a traditional baby name from the dynamic duo of Kim and Kanye; it just wasn't in the cards. Saint West is a name that raises eyebrows and elicits responses across the board.

A more traditional name, like Chad West, probably wouldn't have the same effect. The name has intention, as though the parents have predestined the child to a life of fame (or infamy). Love it or hate it, the name stands out in an increasingly crowded field of celebrity babies.

While every other company in our space is called something like "My Financial Dashboard" or is somehow combined with "analytics," we wanted to find something that stood out and that articulated our unique view on the world. We see things differently than most finance-oriented companies, and we revel in the Zen imagery that goes along with our name. If we had gone the more traditional route, it would have been much more difficult to stand out in a highly competitive landscape.

EMBRACE CONTROVERSY

The financial technology space in which BodeTree operates is stodgy, often dull, and somewhat negative. Most brands focus on the power of being the smartest, most organized, or most powerful. At BodeTree, we fundamentally believe in the concept of business enlightenment. This concept argues that a holistic, balanced, and honest approach to managing a business's finances is the superior path for everyone involved.

The name BodeTree is strange, to be sure, but it's also meant to be controversial. The very message behind the name calls attention to the pervasive challenges that the industry faces and the need that we fill. We're no strangers to controversy, and we are always ready to poke the establishment in the eye when given the opportunity.

ABOVE ALL ELSE, BE MEMORABLE

Getting back to the Kardashian/West clan for just a moment, I'd argue that if the world was heralding the arrival of a celebrity baby named Chad West, odds are that the name would be forgotten in the not-too-distant future (no offense to any Chads out there). Kim and Kanye picked a name that won't be forgotten, giving them (and their management team) opportunities to gain even more exposure for the ever-expanding clan in the future.

The Kardashian management team knows what they're doing, and just as Jay-Z and Beyoncé attempted to trademark their child's name shortly after her birth, I bet we'll be seeing a lot of Saint West™ very soon.

When we chose the name BodeTree, we wanted people to remember our product, team, and mission. Does it explain what we do? Not really. Do people mispronounce it? More than I would care to admit. But, do people forget it? Absolutely not. Even people who have no idea what we do remember who we are, and that's what's important in this day and age.

As for the Kardashians—love them or hate them, they're a shrewd group of businesspeople. How else can you manage to create an empire of fame that is based—essentially—on nothing at all? It's a testament to their brilliant branding—and perhaps a marketing lesson for all entrepreneurs.

IT'S ALL ABOUT THE MODEL

There was once a time when technology reigned supreme and investors flocked to developments that had the potential for scale and monetization. Back then, the marketplace rewarded innovation and experimentation. That time, however, has passed. In today's market, technology takes a back seat to the business model.

Modern entrepreneurs must recognize this shift and position their companies accordingly. Increasingly, the ability to scale quickly is becoming a prerequisite for attracting investment of any kind.

I've been through three fundraising rounds in my career so far. Over the course of our fundraising journey, I've learned a thing or two about what investors want to see.

THE QUEST FOR SCALE

The overwhelming majority of investors today care about only one thing: scale. For those who aren't privy to tech industry lingo, scale simply refers to a company's ability to grow its user or customer base. By gaining scale, companies can use their significant market footprint to give them the room they need to figure out how to monetize their product.

Investors are not interested in slick technology that doesn't lend itself to quick adoption. When my team and I first launched BodeTree, we found ourselves with a great technology that lacked a strong distribution channel. While there was no doubt that software provided a huge benefit to our customers, our direct-to-consumer business model did not lend itself to scaling.

Attracting and retaining small businesses was akin to hand-to-hand combat, and potential investors recognized that fact. A quick lesson in the harsh realities of the venture-capital market taught us that we needed to focus on how to scale before we could raise money.

Ultimately, this process led us to our institutional sales strategy. Rather than sell directly to small businesses, we chose to sell through large institutional partners like banks. This was a fundamental shift to how we did business, but it provided us with the one thing we desperately needed: a clear path to scale.

Instead of winning over businesses one at a time, now we could focus on individual sales relationships that would result in tens of thousands of potential users. Our core technology remained the same, but our business model evolved. Investors soon took notice, and we went on to raise over $5 million in our first two rounds.

THE NEED FOR SPEED

Fixing our business model was a huge step in the right direction, but it was not a panacea. We still had a significant problem on our hands: speed. We had a path to scale, but it was slow and painful.

Our slow but steady pace has proven to be an ongoing thorn in my side. Investors, acquirers, and other strategic partners value speed almost as much as they value the ability to scale. The fatal flaw of BodeTree's model was that the tremendous access our institutional channel provided often came at the cost of an eighteen-month sales cycle.

At first, I felt as though there was not much we could do to fix this. After all, banks are not typically nimble organizations. They move on a geologic time scale when compared to start-ups, and I've learned that all the effort in the world cannot change such a deep-seated behavior.

Fortunately, we managed to improve our situation not by changing the banks but by changing ourselves. We shifted our focus from partners to our own people. By hiring a sales team with experience in the financial and banking space, we cut our sales cycle down by about two-thirds in most cases. It still takes a long time to sell to banks, but we're nowhere near the eighteen-month timeline we used to see.

IT ALL COMES DOWN TO DISTRIBUTION

When I think back to the early days of BodeTree, I'm embarrassed by my naïveté. I truly believed that our innovative technology would be enough to attract customers and investors alike.

Now, six years and many battle scars later, I understand that distribution matters more than technology. Investors seek out businesses that scale rapidly, and if your company hasn't solved for those two variables, you're going to have a tough time raising capital.

THE LAWS OF COFOUNDER ATTRACTION

The cofounder relationship is one of the most important and potentially challenging relationships an entrepreneur will ever have. Not only does it set the tone for the culture that your organization will develop over time, but it also has a tremendous effect on your personal happiness and success.

I've been fortunate in that my relationship with my cofounder has grown steadily stronger over the six years we've worked together. There are ups and downs (as with any relationship), but three guiding principles have helped us grow as entrepreneurs and overcome any challenges that come our way.

SEEK OUT COMPLEMENTARY SKILLS

Anyone with an ounce of entrepreneurial ambition has probably considered going into business with a friend. There are certainly examples of successful businesses started by friends (take Ben and Jerry, for example, or Harley and Davidson), but more often than not, it's the entrepreneurial equivalent of "We should start a band!"

An idea may sound awesome in the moment, but that doesn't mean there's a solid foundation for future success. It isn't enough to have a common interest—successful cofounders must have complementary skills.

My cofounder, Matt Ankrum, brought years of experience as a corporate executive and portfolio manager to the table. His background and skills have been instrumental in helping guide the company through large partnerships and multiple fundraising rounds. We collaborate on all major decisions, such as hiring and product development, but we don't step on each other's toes when it comes to running the business. Too often, when people start a business with a friend, they find themselves occupying the same space because they have similar backgrounds. That brings us to the next principle.

CLEARLY DEFINE ROLES

Unless cofounders have clearly defined roles, conflict is almost inevitable. There are few things more destructive than cofounders who have markedly different views on the company and where it's going. When that conflict plays out in public, the morale and productivity of the entire team can drop precipitously. We experienced this firsthand at BodeTree. Cofounder conflicts that we had were innocent enough in their nature but were painful nevertheless. More often than not, they resulted when someone who had good intentions tried to help guide an initiative without having all the background information.

Matt and I have overcome this challenge by clearly defining the roles we play and, even more important, continually revisiting them to make sure they're still appropriate for the direction the company is taking. This isn't a matter of one person's "owning" a particular area of the business to the exclusion of the other. Rather, it's a matter of knowing with whom the responsibility for a given decision rests.

We make sure to consult each other and talk through the pros and cons of the situation before moving forward, but ultimately, we both agree to respect the final decision that the individual makes. It can be a little difficult for a type A entrepreneur to accept, but we've found that it's the only way to accomplish things quickly and without conflict.

MUTUALLY PLAN FOR THE FUTURE

As a business matures, leadership needs change. The scrappy cofounder structure that worked well in the early days, over time, gives way to a more nuanced approach. More often than not, a business needs a single operational leader who can streamline day-to-day decisions and activities. In a cofounder scenario, one person generally gravitates toward this role while the other will find different ways of remaining engaged. Sometimes, one cofounder settles into an oversight role on the board. Other times, people will revert to their areas of expertise, such as development or sales. Regardless of what transpires, it's important to address these evolutionary changes together and find a solution that works best for the company.

WORK WITH SOMEONE YOU TRUST, RESPECT, AND ADMIRE

The most important business advice I've ever received actually came from my cofounder. When summarizing his business philosophy, he said, "Just be sure to always surround yourself with people you trust, respect, and admire. Everything else will fall in line." This advice formed the core of our partnership and has influenced all our subsequent business decisions. No matter how difficult things get or what challenges come our way, I know that our partnership is strong enough to endure because it is grounded in mutual trust, respect, and admiration.

At the end of the day, a cofounder relationship is just that—a relationship. Like any relationship, it requires a commitment to making it work. You can find a cofounder who has complementary skills and a well-defined role, but if you don't trust, respect, and admire the person, you'll be in trouble. If you stay committed to making the partnership work and operate from a place of mutual respect, the cofounder relationship can be successful and rewarding.

CLARITY COMES FIRST

Many things can (and frequently do) go wrong inside a business. Sales fall through, products don't work, team members get frustrated, and clients get upset. While some of these scenarios play out because of outside circumstances, there's often another culprit to blame: lack of clarity.

In any reasonably complex organization, maintaining clarity in all things is of the utmost importance. Without it, organizations quickly come unglued, and little bumps—like an angry client or misinformed employee—turn into mountains. But with busy schedules, seemingly endless task lists, and diverse personnel, creating a smooth flow of communication can be a challenge. Usually no one is to blame—the process itself is. But what can a business owner do to remedy a lack of clear communication?

I've certainly been guilty of providing unclear direction to my team at BodeTree in the past, but I've learned that clarity in thought, word, and deed can be cultivated over time. Clarity is a habit—and, like any habit, it takes constant reinforcement.

REMEMBER THE VALUE OF STORYTELLING

It isn't enough to list out facts and directives for teams. For people to understand with clarity, you have to tell a compelling story. Just think back to fairy tales and fables: the reason we remember tales like that of the three little pigs is because the story was simple and had a clear point. You can use the same tactic inside an organization.

Not every communication has to be a full-length story, but putting your company's mission, strategy, and operational directives into a coherent narrative helps you, your team, and your customers comprehend and remember the key points.

One thing I try to do with my team is to explain my decisions and requests in a story format. I explain the background of the situation, set the stage, and introduce the individuals involved. From there, I move on to the challenge at hand and explore team members' individual roles in what we're trying to accomplish. Finally, I try to conclude by painting a clear picture of the desired outcome and their role in getting there. My goal is to help my team understand context, motivation, and outcome.

TELL, TELL, AND RETELL

It's not enough just to tell a good story to your team—you have to ensure that everyone is telling the same story. If you are having trouble getting your team motivated or connecting with your clients, that doesn't mean that your story is wrong; you just might need more practice. Storytelling is a learned skill.

Early on, my team and I struggled to rally around a consistent version of our company's story. This was because our position in the marketplace has always been complex, with a product that serves both small business and the institutions that they work with. My team members tended to focus on one aspect of our business model rather than the whole story, and that caused strife and confusion when it came to making decisions regarding marketing and product development.

Eventually, the challenge became so severe that we brought in a consultant to help us develop a message that reflected the whole story of the business. Once we had this consistent story, I made sure to reinforce it with the team every chance I got. All this reinforcement and practice paid off, and our storytelling abilities improved dramatically.

CLARITY MUST COME FIRST

Here's the secret about clarity: it takes work to achieve. There is no magic formula for ensuring that people's visions are aligned and that they share a common understanding of the mission or task. The only way to succeed is for all team members, regardless of rank or position, to make sure that clarity comes first in all interactions.

It's the job of the leader to foster clarity, but success is still a team effort. If something isn't clear, it is still the responsibility of individual team members to speak up and try to fix the problem. Organizational clarity is a two-way street; everyone has to participate equally. The most important thing is to make the effort. If you manage to foster a culture of clarity inside of your organization, you'll see fewer problems, better execution, and happier, more productive team members.

STOP DISRUPTING AND START IMPROVING

Hot trends in technology come and go, but their effect on the marketplace and consumer preferences can shape the future in unforeseen ways.

The "social, mobile, local" and "Uber of Everything" movement that has dominated recent conversation has been, at its core, a fundamentally consumer-focused phenomenon. The advent and proliferation of technologies like Facebook, Gmail, and the iPhone have not only changed the way we interact with the world around us but also dramatically changed our expectations of how we can and should interact with technology.

TODAY'S CONSUMERS DEMAND MORE

As consumers, we've become so accustomed to smooth, intuitive, and powerful technology in our personal lives that we're perplexed when we're forced to use systems and products that remain stuck in the last century. We now demand more out of *all* companies and technologies we deal with—not just the "cool" ones.

The central theme we will see play out over the next five to ten years is likely one of improvement versus disruption when it comes to traditional industries. There is a tremendous opportunity for start-ups to succeed by improving existing technology instead of chasing the next major disruption in the marketplace. The last wave of hot start-ups helped introduce a new way of interacting with the world around us. The next wave will take that development one step further by helping the laggards find their place in the new digital world.

Take banking, for example. There have been a number of start-ups in the past few years that have tried, unsuccessfully, to disrupt traditional banking. Simple, a banking start-up that launched in 2009 came closest in its attempt to do away with the physical banking center, but it was acquired by BBVA Bank in 2014 for $117 million and continues to suffer from drawbacks associated with an online-only bank. Rather than try to disrupt the entire banking industry, why not try to help make it better?

WORK WITH THEM, NOT AGAINST THEM

The US banking sector is so entrenched and protected that challenging it from the outside is an exercise in futility. It's highly unlikely that a start-up will come around and pose a real threat to the likes of Bank of America or Chase anytime soon. But there is still a huge opportunity for entrepreneurs to help change the way banks serve their customers.

Consider what it currently takes to get a loan from a mainstream bank. In almost every case, you can count on months of back-and-forth, multiple document requests, and an incredible reliance on traditional underwriting practices. It's only a matter of time before someone figures out how to improve this decades-old process by helping banks adopt some of the approaches pioneered by organizations like Lending Club, Kabbage, and CAN Capital.

Another area that is ripe for improvement rather than disruption is business services. The technology available to small and midsize businesses today still leaves much to be desired. However, like banks, the entrenched players in this arena are strong enough that it's difficult for an outsider to truly alter the status quo. Intuit, the financial technology behemoth, recently articulated its desire to become the "operating system for small business," and I believe it has the right idea.

IT'S ALL ABOUT RELATIONSHIPS

Still, the vision of an interconnected, seamless platform that enables small and midsize businesses to create customized solutions that fit their specific needs remains an ambitious goal. The entire sector stands to benefit if someone can find a way to put the relationship with the business owner at the forefront of the experience and deliver on the promise of a holistic "operating system for business."

Banking and business services are just two of many areas of industry that stand to benefit from the next wave of start-up innovation. The new widespread acceptance of cloud technology and higher demands from consumers means that no one can afford to be just "good enough." The opportunity for start-ups to improve existing industries is immense.

Banking is a multi-trillion-dollar global industry, and business services in the United States alone can be measured in the hundreds of billions of dollars. There's so much room for improvement in these segments that it boggles the mind. Sure, you could spend your time trying to come up with the next big thing to take on the Apple Watch, but why not go after the low-hanging fruit first? When thinking about the next hot trend in start-ups, remember the words of the great American philosopher Huey Lewis: "There is no denyin' that it's hip to be square."

Don't Ignore Obvious Problems

There are many mistakes that you can (and likely will) make as an entrepreneur. From hiring the wrong people to not raising enough capital, the potential pitfalls are numerous. However, there's one mistake that trumps all others: ignoring obvious problems. It sounds like common sense, but this is a mistake that entrepreneurs make time and time again.

Entrepreneurship is a deeply personal journey, and it's often difficult to separate logic from emotion when making decisions. Many times the desire to make a partnership or deal work is so strong that entrepreneurs ignore glaring red flags along the way. Ignoring these obvious problems, however, is never a good solution. Problems don't just disappear. In fact, they tend to grow in severity the longer they're ignored.

Lessons from Greece

There is a lot that entrepreneurs can learn from the handling of the Greek debt crisis. Back in May 2010, the European Central Bank, International Monetary Fund, and the European Commission (collectively known as the Troika) chose to provide a €110 billion bailout to Greece to cover its shortfall. Since that time, the crisis seems to emerge every few years as Greece continuously exhibits further inability to repay its debts. While arguments rage over the morality and economics of continued bailouts and austerity, no one seems to want to address the obvious: the math simply doesn't work. Greece couldn't pay back the debt even in a good economy. Unfortunately for the Troika, the problem has been delayed for so long that overall exposure has ballooned to an estimated €300 billion.

In the case of Greece and the Troika, the core problems were obvious from day one. However, the powers that be chose to ignore real issues and instead kicked the proverbial can down the road. Now those same issues have ballooned to a size that is no longer manageable.

Lessons from BodeTree

We've learned similar lessons at BodeTree. In the past, we've pursued partnerships and opportunities that had potential for tremendous upsides but that were hampered by obvious strategic problems. These issues ranged from partnerships that just didn't align to channels that conflicted with the overall ethos of our solution.

Rather than recognizing and addressing these obvious issues early on, we allowed ourselves to be blinded by the opportunity and moved forward in the hope that they would simply go away. Naturally, the issues only grew until the opportunity no longer made sense for the organization.

In retrospect, we should have dealt with those issues much earlier in the process. Like the Troika, we were so caught up in the big-picture strategy and short-term maneuverings that we lost sight of the obvious. Whether Greece can't pay back a debt or a product integration just doesn't make sense, obvious problems don't go away. They only get worse with time.

The lesson here is that problems should be addressed as they arise. Sometimes that means that a particular opportunity is a nonstarter, but more often than not, identifying and addressing issues early on lead to more innovative solutions. Perhaps if the Troika had been able to recognize Greece's inability to pay its debts earlier on, it could have found a better solution to the crisis rather than simply committing to bailout after bailout.

Similarly, my team could likely have salvaged some of these misaligned opportunities and reached a mutually beneficial solution for everyone involved. Regardless of what could have been, the important thing is that we have learned our lesson and now have a much better strategy for dealing with problems.

"Fake It until You Make It" Rarely Pays Off

We live in a world where "fake it until you make it" has become a commonplace behavior, especially for entrepreneurs. Start-up founders in particular face incredible pressure to look like an overnight success, which can lead them down a dangerous path of deception. However, I've found that the short-term benefits of deception, no matter how small, always give way to larger headaches and challenges.

We All Face the Temptation to Exaggerate and Deceive

The temptation to present oneself in a different and potentially better light can be strong. After all, creating something from nothing can be a Herculean effort, and most entrepreneurs will do whatever it takes to help that process along—even if it means stretching the truth from time to time.

Early on, I used to joke about how often we encountered "truthiness" in the marketplace. "Truthiness" refers to making statements that are accurate in spirit if not in fact. Often, we'd notice representatives of partner companies squirming when they described the number of customers they had or what their technology could do. I myself struggled with the temptation to overstate technical ability during the first few years.

Our development team was moving so quickly that sometimes it was easy to describe features that were in process as being already available. The trouble was that whenever I ended up overcommitting on the product-development front, I ended up creating unnecessary stress and anxiety as we rushed to live up to what was promised. At the end of the day, any near-term benefits I gained from presenting my product as something it wasn't were outmatched by the stress that always accompanies "truthiness."

The Truth Always Comes Out

No matter how good your intentions may be or how innocent your deception seems at the time, the truth always comes out. I learned this firsthand when we launched an early partnership at BodeTree. At the time, our

41

distributions strategy focused primarily on a single institutional partner. Its team insisted that it had a network of clients and was ripe for third parties such as those BodeTree could leverage.

We poured ourselves into trying to serve this market but never found the type of success we desired. We agonized for months over our product, marketing, and strategy, desperate to figure out where we had gone wrong. It was only after talking to other partners that we realized that the number of customers the partner served was much smaller than we had been led to believe.

It wasn't that our partner's assertions were completely wrong or ill intended. It was just that our partner presented a version of reality that was based more on hope than on facts. Once the truth came out, we were able to revise our strategy accordingly and move forward. Our relationship with the partner remained intact, but the level of trust was never quite the same.

AUTHENTICITY IS MORE POWERFUL THAN DECEPTION

The most important virtue I can encourage in my team is authenticity. I'm always amazed at how understanding and forgiving people can be when you simply tell the truth and work hard to do what is right. It isn't always easy, but in the end, authenticity wins out over deception every time. At BodeTree, we simply tell our story to prospective clients, partners, and investors. We focus on the positive but never shy away from being forthright and earnest about our challenges and limitations. This authenticity builds trust, and trust builds lasting partnerships.

That's why I encourage my team members and all the entrepreneurs I advise to strive for honesty and authenticity in everything they do. The temptation to exaggerate or bend the truth can be strong, but it never pays off. In this world, a person's word and reputation are all he or she truly has. Once that reputation has been compromised, it can never be fully restored.

DEVELOPING YOUR PRODUCT

WHEN TO ACCEPT TECHNICAL DEBT AND WHEN TO PAY IT OFF

Being an entrepreneurial leader is all about making decisions and learning to accept trade-offs. When you're responsible for an entire organization, there's virtually no way to balance the various needs of your team perfectly. Everyone has to learn to compromise in order to move forward, and sometimes that means accepting temporary fixes.

In the world of software development, these temporary fixes are often referred to as "technical debt." Technical debt is unavoidable to some degree. While technical debt isn't inherently good or bad, there is a time and a place for accepting it, and there are situations in which it must be paid off rapidly. The key for leaders is to recognize the nuance of each situation and make wise decisions about managing this debt.

WHAT IS TECHNICAL DEBT?

Much like credit card debt, technical debt often solves an immediate need but carries with it some long-term ramifications. Similarly, if left unchecked, it has the tendency to compound over time and become unmanageable. Simply put, technical debt is the result of developmental shortcuts or near-term product decisions that solve a need but that might not be the best solution in the long term.

We've accrued our fair share of technical debt over the years at BodeTree. Since our inception in 2010, we've pivoted and refined our offering to find our product/market fit. That process has required us to experiment, adjust, and iterate—and every step of that leaves its mark on the code.

WHEN SHOULD I ACCEPT TECHNICAL DEBT?

Technical debt isn't always a bad thing, and entrepreneurs shouldn't be scared of it. When you're an early-stage company, you almost never have a perfect understanding of your market's needs—that takes time and hands-on learning, as well as multiple pivots, to get right. Accepting technical debt is simply part of doing business, and it can help you build the right product for your market.

Entrepreneurs should be willing to accept technical debt in three scenarios. First, quick adjustments and iterative development work well when you're dealing with your first big customer. Moving speedily in these scenarios enables you to quickly refine the product and test feedback.

Second, technical debt is acceptable when you're looking to build out a minimally viable product and have yet to secure funding. Development work is costly no matter how you look at it. When you're bootstrapping, you don't necessarily have the luxury of rewriting large chunks of already-working code. Accruing technical debt can hold you over until you're in a position to spend.

Finally, I believe it's acceptable to make quick fixes when testing new features in an established product. Sometimes the killer new feature you introduce simply isn't a good fit or isn't well received by your customers. Moving quickly and accepting that you might have to go back and change things later helps you focus on the things that are truly important and cut your losses quickly if it doesn't work out.

When Should I Pay It Off?

There comes a time when the technical debt that has built up over the years begins to hamper the performance of your product and the effectiveness of your team. When you find yourself at that point, it's time to pay off your balance. We reached that point about a year and a half ago at BodeTree. Making changes to the product became increasingly difficult for us because so many of the features were interconnected. We were loath to make any sweeping changes, fearing that they might have unintended consequences.

For BodeTree, the ultimate signal came when we found our product/market fit. The institutions that we sell through (primarily banks and other financial institutions) started adopting the product in droves, and the small businesses they served found success using our system. We identified what was working and what elements of the product were not being used. This freed us to cut the things that were inactive and focus on improving the performance and stability of the things that were.

This approach enabled us to conserve capital and make the right product decisions for the business. Had we attempted to pay off our technical debt sooner, we likely wouldn't have known where to focus our efforts.

Every product-focused company has technical debt of some kind. If used properly, it can help your business move quickly and mature toward product/market fit. However, if left unchecked for too long, technical debt can make your product unmanageable for your customers and team alike. The key is in finding balance—every business is different, and it's up to the leaders to identify the right balance of technical debt for their organization.

ESSENTIALISM IS KEY

Whether you're running your own business or managing a team, it's easy to fall victim to decision fatigue. Leaders face so many stressors and decision points throughout the day that at some point the quality of decisions begins to deteriorate rapidly.

There is a common but false belief held by many in the entrepreneurial community that strength of will is the key to avoiding the effects of decision fatigue. Strong leaders, many believe, can simply muscle through fatigue and continue making good decisions. I argue that this belief couldn't be further from the truth.

I've struggled with decision fatigue at many points throughout my career, but lately I have felt its effect on my life more acutely. Leading a company in hypergrowth mode, raising capital, and balancing the demands of private life have taken their toll. Rather than descend into a stress spiral or pretend that I can simply muscle through things, I decided to look deeper into the problem and find a solution. That solution, it turns out, is a concept known as essentialism.

THERE ARE NO *EASY* ANSWERS, BUT THERE *ARE* SIMPLE ANSWERS

One of my favorite quotes comes from President Ronald Reagan, who remarked, "There are no easy answers, but there are simple answers." It's easy to forget this fact when you're in the weeds of running a business, but it holds true in many instances, and this simplicity is at the core of essentialism.

The concept of essentialism, which can be traced back to the works of Aristotle and Plato, holds that a given entity has a few core traits that define its very existence. There can be many additional traits, but there are always a few that define the core of the entity in question.

This seemingly abstract concept actually simplifies the decision-making process and can be quite helpful for leaders who are trying to avoid fatigue and burnout. When you apply essentialist thought to a problem, you actively strip it down to its most basic aspects. Shedding extraneous information helps you focus your thoughts, get down to the point, and simplify the decision-making process.

START WITH YOUR GOD PARTICLE

I've talked about finding your company's God Particle, the ethos of your business and the ideal that colors everything you do. Identifying and embracing these core values is central to simplifying the decision-making process. It provides you with a starting point and helps answer some important questions, including this one: "Is this consistent with my ethics, strategy, and end goal?"

Starting with your God Particle enables you to approach decisions and challenges with specificity and purpose. If a decision results in something that is inconsistent with your God Particle, you know you're making a mistake.

At BodeTree, our God Particle is the liberation of data through authentic human interaction. We believe that great things can be accomplished through data, but only if that data comes from genuine, simple, and authentic interactions with the small businesses we serve. If I know that a given path would run counter to these values, I move in the other direction. This confidence of character takes a tremendous burden off my shoulders as a decision maker.

HOW TO BUILD AN ESSENTIALIST FRAMEWORK FOR DECISION MAKING

The only way to avoid decision fatigue is to simplify the decision process so that it is quick, straightforward, and effective. By embracing essentialism, you can break the process down into a few steps, evaluate the situation, and make that decision quickly and confidently. Here are the three simple steps I use:

Step One: determine whether the situation at hand is consistent with your core values. If it isn't, don't do it. It's as simple as that.

Step Two: identify the likely outcome and worst-case scenario. If you can get comfortable with how you think things will play out and can accept the worst-case scenario, move forward.

Step Three: determine how the decision will affect your resources (time, people, and money). Is the benefit worth the cost? If you think it is, move forward—and don't second-guess yourself. You might end up being wrong, but worrying about past decisions will only drive you crazy. Accept the decision, and keep moving forward.

We all suffer from decision fatigue from time to time. After all, we are inundated with information, anxieties, and stresses in almost every aspect of our life. In spite of all that, it's important to remember that there are no *easy* answers—but there *are* simple answers. Essentialism is the path to simplification, and it is a great tool for today's overwhelmed entrepreneurs.

IKEA CAN TEACH YOU A LOT ABOUT USER EXPERIENCE

In an increasingly complex and unequal world, there is one experience that is almost universal, speaking to both the agony and the ecstasy of the human experience. I'm talking of course, about the assembly of Ikea furniture.

We all know the story: you spot an affordable, well-designed piece of furniture while you're wandering through the labyrinth that is an Ikea store, and you have a moment of weakness. Perhaps it's the prospect of leaving with a shiny new object or the allure of post-checkout-line Swedish meatball samples that drives you to purchase. Whatever the reason, you end up buying a piece of furniture that fits neatly in a flat box and take it home.

Of course, that's when things get interesting. I've assembled more than my fair share of Ikea furniture, and I can't help but think about user experience when I'm going through the process. Every time, I have walked away from the experience with new and mostly assembled furniture—and a healthy new respect for the importance of user experience.

REMEMBER THAT PERCEPTION IS OFTEN REALITY

There's nothing quite like the feeling of dread that washes over you when you open up the box containing your new furniture and approximately forty-eight thousand different screws, washers, and bolts pour out. When that happens, you unintentionally make a snap judgment that colors the entire experience going forward. Regardless of whether the actual assembly ends up being easier than you expect, your entire user experience is colored by this initial perception.

We dealt with a similar phenomenon early on at BodeTree. When we launched the first version of our product in 2011, we required our prospective users to fill out a laundry list of items before they could use the tool. Looking back on the process, I'm embarrassed by our terrible user experience.

Even though the actual data we were requesting was light by most standards, we presented it in such a way that it instantly felt overwhelming.

That put our users in a bad mood right off the bat, and as a result, they were extraordinarily unforgiving once they were using the product.

PROVIDE THE USER WITH ALL THE NECESSARY TOOLS

Ikea is great at giving you almost everything you need to assemble its furniture, but it seems as if no matter what I do, I always end up missing a random bolt, screw, or hex key. Regardless of whether it's my fault for losing it or Ikea's for not including it, the experience of hitting a roadblock because you don't have the tools you need is insanely frustrating.

People hate uncertainty, especially when it comes to interacting with products. There's an expectation that the user will be provided with everything needed to use a product, as well as instructions for moving forward.

When we introduced our loan builder product at BodeTree, we discovered just how important setting user expectations truly are. Our goal was to streamline the loan application process for small businesses— something that usually takes weeks or months and that can be incredibly tedious. Instead of providing people with everything they needed to move smoothly through the process of applying for a loan, we threw them curveballs at random intervals.

The worst of these was on step six of our process, when we prompted the user to upload his or her tax return. The problem was that the user didn't know that he or she needed to have a tax return handy, let alone in convenient PDF form. We learned quickly that we needed to make all requirements known to the user well in advance in order to avoid frustration and abandonment. While we had the vision of a "simplified process," our initial version did not deliver on these expectations; as a result, the overall user experience suffered.

WHEN IN DOUBT, OVEREXPLAIN

Perhaps the most frustrating misstep in user experience is lack of explanation. My team and I realized over time that one of the biggest obstacles to creating a solid user experience is lack of clarity on how to proceed. Think of those expletive-inducing Ikea-assembly moments when you're sure you've done everything properly, yet the table is still wobbly, or the shelf isn't level: How much frustration could have been avoided if the instructions had just mentioned that you did, in fact, need to drill a hole? Quite a bit, I wager.

If there is an outside chance that a step or instruction within your user experience could be perceived as unclear, it's better to overexplain. Doing so is the easiest way to ensure that your customers can accomplish their goals without excess heartache. Taking a step back from your product for a moment and adopting the perspective of the user is an illuminating experience that can make a massive difference for both you and your customers.

BEWARE THE 5 PERCENT PROBLEM

The only thing that the public loves more than building up a hero is tearing one down. The history of Silicon Valley is littered with start-ups that went from hero to zero. One such case is that of Evernote, the Icarus-like productivity app that took off to great acclaim and then fell back to earth.

Back in 2013, Evernote was yet another Silicon Valley darling with a $1 billion valuation. Since that time, Evernote has struggled to generate profits and maintain its traction with users. Part of the problem was that Evernote suffered from feature overload that obscured its core value proposition and confused users.

This story struck a chord with me on a personal level. BodeTree suffered from the very same feature-bloat problem that plagued Evernote. It took us a full year of introspection and more than a few difficult decisions to fix the problem. The struggle we went through taught me one of the most important lessons of my entrepreneurial journey: if you can't easily explain what your product does, you have a problem.

THE 5 PERCENT PROBLEM

If you're looking for the reason why Evernote stumbled, you need only look back at a 2013 interview conducted with Evernote CEO Phil Libin. Over the course of the conversation, Libin conceded that Evernote had so many features that it was often difficult to explain to newcomers.

"What winds up happening at Evernote conferences is that people go and they say, 'Oh, I love Evernote and I've been using it for years and now I realize I've only been using it for 5 percent of what it can do, and the problem is that it's a different 5 percent for everyone.' If everyone just found the same 5 percent, then we'd just cut the other 95 percent and save ourselves a lot of money. It's a very broad usage base."

This is called the "5 percent problem," and it is a major issue for the industry. Around the same time, BodeTree was going through something very similar. If you surveyed our users (and we did—frequently), you'd find that everyone had a different perception of the core value that BodeTree provided. While every feature held value, there were so many that we struggled to present a cohesive view of what BodeTree was.

LEARNING TO SAY NO

My team and I never set out to build a feature-heavy product. Our problem was that early on we were afraid to say no to potential clients and partners. We were largely an unproven product, and when an attractive partner asked for a feature, we often obliged. This approach, of course, led to costly overruns and a somewhat bloated product.

Eventually, the team and I gained enough confidence and traction to begin to say no to unnecessary feature requests that came our way. It wasn't easy, because we still desired to please everyone who we encountered, but over time, it paid off. We focused our efforts on refining our core experience. As we did, it became far easier to explain what the product did and how it would benefit our potential clients.

MAKING A CHOICE

If you're an entrepreneur who struggles with the 5 percent problem, fear not. You can fix your situation quickly, just as we did at BodeTree. The first step is to learn to say no. The next step, however, is to make a choice. Entrepreneurs must decide what their core experience is and commit to it. At BodeTree, we decided to focus on solving the challenge facing small businesses by automatically organizing banking transactions into financial accounting.

Once you reaffirm your commitment to your product's core experience, you can move to either eliminate or demote noncore features. We eliminated numerous features, including roles, profiles, internal messaging, and various customizations. This decision streamlined our codebase and dramatically improved our performance.

The 5 percent problem that plagued both Evernote and BodeTree should never be underestimated or ignored. Only products that have a clear focus and an easy-to-understand value proposition can survive in today's crowded marketplace. Entrepreneurs must learn to say no to feature requests no matter how painful doing so may be. From there, they must make a choice and focus on a single core experience and those features that support it. Only in doing so can companies overcome the 5 percent problem and thrive.

SOMETIMES YOU HAVE TO CREATE YOUR MARKET

The world is littered with the ashes of innovative and often superior products that never really caught on. The companies behind these products failed because they created something that the existing market wasn't prepared to accept and use. They tried to fit a square peg into a round hole when in reality they should have focused on simply creating the round hole. It isn't always enough to create an innovative product; sometimes you have to create the market.

I found myself in this very position a few years ago shortly after launching our product. BodeTree was designed to be the go-to financial operating system for small businesses, instantly organizing, analyzing, and interpreting their data and transforming it into something actionable. We didn't have many direct competitors at launch (and still don't). At first I viewed this lack of competition as a real advantage. However, I quickly came to realize that there wasn't a preexisting market for the solution we created.

We knew that companies that used our product saved both time and money and were categorically better off than companies that did not. We had created something incredibly valuable that people needed, but they simply didn't know that they needed it.

THE CUSTOMER ISN'T ALWAYS RIGHT

Customers weren't looking for our product. In fact, customers weren't even aware that such a product existed. They were conditioned to think about their financial needs in the context of traditional accounting, which had been the only option available to them for the past twenty-five years.

One of my favorite (probably apocryphal) quotes from Henry Ford says, "If I had asked people what they wanted, they would have said faster horses." People thought they wanted a product that did away with all the little annoyances they experienced with existing financial management solutions. They thought they wanted a faster horse. But what they were looking for was a fresh approach that addressed the root of their problems; they just didn't know it yet.

SELL THE INNOVATION, NOT THE PRODUCT

Stuart Butterfield, the founder of the incredibly popular group chat service Slack, recently published an internal memo that he circulated to his team back in 2013 ahead of their launch. In it, he outlined a problem very similar to that which we experienced at BodeTree. His solution was to "sell the innovation, not the product."

Simply put, his strategy was to sell people on all the ways that their lives would be improved through the use of Slack rather than selling the merits of the individual features. He realized that if he tried to sell features, people would draw the wrong conclusions, make poor comparisons, or simply ignore the message.

He flipped the traditional conversation on its head and sold the concept of organizational transformation rather than communication tool. The software was simply the means to achieve the transformation.

By helping people understand and aspire to achieve something more meaningful, the Slack team was able to change the conversation and create a new and highly receptive market. The move shifted people's understanding of their needs and broke them out of their preconditioned view of existing. This strategy was as difficult as it was risky, but the payoff proved to be immense.

We did something similar at BodeTree. Instead of selling a great financial management tool, we sold the idea that peace, tranquility, and enlightenment could be achieved for stressed-out small-business owners.

We knew that people hated finance and accounting. It was a constant source of anxiety and stress—mostly because of fear, complex numbers, and a general lack of understanding about the financial story. But we told the story of a future in which that anxiety gave way to confidence and understanding—with BodeTree at the center of the plot. Almost overnight, we found that this simple strategy shift opened up a tremendous market that no one had known existed. People craved peace and financial enlightenment, and we were there to provide it.

Focus on Equal Parts Storytelling and Execution

Telling a story that opens the eyes of your target customers is only half the battle. Finding the right emotional hook changes the dynamic of how your product is positioned and unlocks previously hidden markets, but you still have to deliver that emotion to your customers.

For Slack, that delivery means constant focus on making its solution the easiest and smoothest experience possible. For BodeTree, it means taking the fear out of finance. We have a maniacal focus on user experience at every level. Creating a market isn't worth anything if your product isn't able to serve it effectively. For an innovative company to be successful, it has to focus on storytelling and execution in equal measure.

The Innovator's Dilemma

Innovators face a very real risk every time they broach a new topic, disrupt an industry, or even tweak their product. The market may not be ready—and if it's not, then failure is always an option. The real innovation is not always developing the app, the gadget, or the software; sometimes it's changing how people think and behave—and that's the biggest (and best) challenge of all.

THE ADORABLE PUPPY PRINCIPLE

In mid-2015, a member of my team posted a video to YouTube that showed his two adorable puppies, Colby and Bleu (collectively known as "The Cheeses"), rushing to their food bowls week after week over the course of a whole year. Throughout the video's one-and-a-half-minute run time, viewers can see the puppies grow up before their eyes. Within four hours of the video's posting, it had already racked up nearly three million views and garnered attention from companies looking to license its content.

All this sudden attention made me think about how I connect with my own clients. Over the past five years, I've spent thousands of hours and incredible sums of money trying to market our product to the millions of small-business owners in the United States. I've landed coverage in major publications, shared our story on national television numerous times, and engaged some of the brightest consultants I could find. We've had success for sure, but we've never seen anything take off like the video of "The Cheeses."

After watching the video for what seemed like the hundredth time, I had an epiphany of sorts. No matter how hard you work to refine your company's message and marketing, unless you manage to connect with people on a basic emotional level, you'll always find yourself fighting an uphill battle. I call it the Adorable Puppy Principle.

MARKETING IS ALMOST NEVER ABOUT LOGIC

The puppy video works so well because it elicits feelings of joy, nostalgia, and excitement. It speaks to people's basic emotions.

There's a running joke at BodeTree about finding new taglines for our product. My team and I have gone through hundreds of tags, and no matter what we come up with, we always find ourselves back to square one within a matter of months. Each time we try, we make a perfectly cogent argument outlining the reasons why people should care and how they can take action. Still, we've never found something that resonated exactly the way we want.

Thanks to the Cheeses, I realized the underlying reason is that we've never managed to tap into people's basic needs. This isn't a new idea by any means, but it's one, I think, that technology companies—particularly those in the financial space—can easily forget. I know that I certainly did. In our marketing, we vacillated between abstract messages and the extremely tactical, but each time we failed to tap into the primal elements of the human mind.

PUTTING THE ADORABLE PUPPY PRINCIPLE TO WORK

The video of the puppies is all about love. The mere fact that it was compiled over the course of a year speaks to the joy that the Cheeses bring to their humans. I could easily see it serving as a commercial for any pet-focused company. After all, if that company's ethos is that pets are an important part of the family experience, then what better way to advertise than to remind people of the joy that pets can bring?

Some products lend themselves to emotion-based marketing. Others are harder to adapt. BodeTree is a financial management platform for small business, which doesn't exactly lend itself to the unadulterated joy of watching puppies race around. Still, I'm going to make sure that my team and I learn from this experience. I'm convinced that any company with a product or service worth selling can find ways to establish powerful emotional connections with their customers.

Perhaps the trick to applying the Adorable Puppy Principle in marketing is to focus your efforts on uncovering your product's ethos. Once you know what your product or company stands for, you can start to connect back to the underlying emotional need that it satisfies.

The experience of watching this video go viral has been eye opening and enlightening. It has inspired me to take a much deeper look at my product's ethos and messaging. It's time for us to put the Adorable Puppy Principle to work. I now know that we can do a better job of connecting with our customers—it just took two adorable puppies to help me realize it.

GETTING NOTICED

EMBRACE CONTROVERSY

Every start-up wants to "go viral" at some point. After all, who wouldn't want free, widespread publicity? The problem, however, is that viral marketing is easier said than done. Viral marketing is a finicky beast and one that hinges on the perfect combination of timing, authenticity, and luck.

One entrepreneur who managed to go viral is Candice Galek, founder of Bikini Luxe, an online swimwear retailer. Bikini Luxe does much of its marketing via traditional social media platforms, including Facebook and Pinterest. However, it was Candice's decision to focus on LinkedIn that turned heads.

Now, LinkedIn isn't typically the venue that comes to mind when one thinks of bikinis and bikini models. However, Candice recognized the opportunity to connect with potential investors, partners, and customers and decided to use the platform.

She began by posting images of her products being modeled by Miss Universe contender Natalie Roser and other models with the caption "Is this appropriate for LinkedIn?"

"The goal was to test the waters and start a conversation," said Candice. "I didn't expect there to be such a tremendous response or controversy."

The post, however, generated an incredible amount of attention, garnering more than fifty thousand views and five hundred comments (both positive and negative) while increasing her number of LinkedIn followers by over thirty thousand.

After talking with Candice and reflecting on her story, I realized just how difficult it can be to ride the wave of viral marketing. At BodeTree, the team and I have tried to be controversial and go viral at various points in time, but we have never made it as big as Bikini Luxe has (due in no small part to our position in the financial industry versus the swimwear industry).

Candice, on the other hand, has done an excellent job of taking advantage of this "lightning in a bottle" moment. Bikini Luxe's website traffic from LinkedIn now rivals that coming from Pinterest, and sales have spiked dramatically. There are certainly some entrepreneurial lessons to be learned from Candice's story.

LESSON ONE: CULTIVATE CONTROVERSY WITH NUANCE

People who try to "go viral" by being intentionally controversial usually fail. The public has a nose for contrived, forced efforts, and it responds with disdain. (The "scary singing clown" campaign that Kabbage released a few years ago comes to mind.) Still, relatively few things go viral without some intention. The key to success is a nuanced approach that looks natural but that still has intention behind it.

Intentional or not, Candice struck the perfect balance in her LinkedIn posts. The images themselves weren't overt or pornographic, but they certainly went beyond the buttoned-up norm for LinkedIn. This balance allowed for a genuine conversation that drove people to engage rather than disregard. Had she pushed the boundaries too far at the outset, I believe she would have been written off right away.

LESSON TWO: ENGAGE CONTROVERSY WITH INTELLIGENCE AND GRACE

When Candice's posts on LinkedIn started to go viral, the social network's content algorithm kicked in, proactively deleting her post and profile picture without her notice. Rather than reach out in righteous indignation, however, Candice chose to engage intelligently with the team at LinkedIn.

After speaking to high-level employees of the company on a near-daily basis, Candice managed to get all her posts and pictures put back in place. In fact, she now has her own follow button, and her posts now generate almost as much engagement as well-known business leaders like Sir Richard Branson and Bill Gates.

Had Candice reacted with anger or rage, the response would likely have been much different. Instead, she recognized that this wave of controversy could benefit her business if she responded with grace. As a result, she gained an almost overnight presence on LinkedIn that rivals that of well-established business icons.

LESSON THREE: MAKE THE MOST OF THE OPPORTUNITIES THAT COME YOUR WAY

Once her company went viral, Candice was inundated with connection requests and opportunities. Rather than let these simply pass by, she has embraced them with gusto. She recognized this as a once-in-a-business opportunity and is now getting the most out of it.

Throughout this process, she has connected with fellow entrepreneurs, investors, and media personalities. She has been able to leverage these connections to secure her very own column in *Inc. Magazine* and become a LinkedIn Influencer.

The great "LinkedIn Bikini Controversy of 2016" is a valuable lesson for entrepreneurs of all kinds. Controversy, if handled with nuance and grace, can be a great way to jumpstart a conversation in the most unlikely of venues. Whether it was intentional or not, Candice and the team at Bikini Luxe have managed this situation with a skill and aplomb that most marketers can only dream of attaining.

LEVERAGE THE POWER OF THE CROWD

I'll be the first to admit that when it comes to the holidays, I'm a last-minute shopper. My procrastination in the gift-purchasing department is never intentional. It's just that between raising a young family, running a growing business, and writing for publications like *Forbes*, I just don't have much time to spare.

So it seems as if every Christmas Eve I find myself part of the frenzied crowd of other last-minute shoppers, scrambling to get everything done in time. In 2015, however, instead of getting frustrated with the crowds, I looked to them for overall inspiration. As I made my way through the throngs of people, I couldn't help but think of the power of the crowd, particularly when it comes to crowdsourcing.

My fascination with the concept of crowdsourcing started back in 2004, as it did for many who read James Surowiecki's brilliant book *The Wisdom of Crowds*. The idea that the collective wisdom of a large group could prove superior to the expertise of individuals is powerful. This has been proven out to a large degree by experiments both large and small. However, for the longest time, I wondered about the commercial aspects of collective wisdom. There's no doubt that crowdsourcing has plenty of technical applications, from prediction markets to market intelligence. While there is certainly immense value to be found in those applications, I was more interested in how it would affect the small-business economy.

Fortunately, in the years since I first encountered the concept, many solutions have emerged that can help small businesses and start-ups leverage the crowd to solve problems they face on a daily basis and punch well above their weight in the market.

LOOK TO THE CROWD FOR CONTENT

For a small enterprise, developing and running a comprehensive marketing campaign can be a gargantuan task. Business owners are so busy trying to keep up with day-to-day operations that the idea of sitting down to draft content or test new ideas seems laughable. Fortunately, busy entrepreneurs can look to existing and prospective customers to help create content and share it socially.

Crowdsourcing articles, social media, and video can help small-business owners cultivate a rich and diverse library of meaningful content related to their business while also getting their customers to engage personally with the brand. This very book is a great example of the power of crowdsourced content with its collection of guest contributors. When your customers engage in the creation of content, they become more personally connected than you could ever achieve with traditional marketing.

BUILD LOYALTY WITH PEER-TO-PEER SUPPORT
To stay relevant in today's highly competitive market, it's incredibly important for small businesses and start-ups to offer amazing, personalized customer support. However, just as with marketing, it can be difficult for entrepreneurs to devote enough time to dealing with customer questions and concerns when they're busy trying to keep their heads above water. Again, with the advent of crowdsourcing, small-business owners can look to their existing customer base for the solution.

By creating a robust forum where current customers can help one another overcome challenges and answer questions, you can deliver a fantastic service experience while instilling a strong sense of loyalty in your base—a process that has already been adopted by large companies like Apple to great acclaim.

LOOK TO THE CROWD FOR DIVERSE FUNDING OPTIONS
Securing funding from traditional lenders can be a difficult and trying process. However, by crowdsourcing the search for funding, small businesses and start-ups can access the capital that works for them quicker and easier than ever before. Crowdsourced funding has the luxury of offering a greater variety of solutions to meet the needs of individual borrowers, due in part to less stringent regulatory standards.

For people looking to raise money for charitable causes or when appealing to the crowd's altruistic side, there is GoFundMe, which allows people to pledge donations of any size. For entrepreneurs looking to simultaneously validate a concept and fund early development, there are solutions like Kickstarter and Indiegogo. Finally, for individuals and companies looking for debt financing, there are companies like Kabbage, LendingClub, and Dealstruck. All these providers offer solutions that would not have been possible fifteen years ago and that still seem wildly out of reach for traditional financial institutions to offer. Put simply, since the crowdfunders aren't hampered by tradition, they have more opportunities to offer a solution that works for those seeking capital.

It's certainly an exciting day and age for small businesses and start-ups. Never before have entrepreneurs been able to leverage technology, their customers, and one another so effectively to accomplish so much with so little. The wisdom and resourcefulness of the crowd has the potential to change dramatically the way that small businesses and start-ups operate worldwide. By taking advantage of technology and the wisdom of the crowd, small companies and start-ups have the opportunity to level the playing field, competing on par with their larger counterparts, more aggressively than ever before.

HOW TO GET PRESS WITHOUT A PUBLIC RELATIONS AGENCY

Building and managing a media presence can be invaluable for small businesses and start-ups. Media coverage can help your company stand out and attract potential customers, investors, and business partners. Getting media attention, however, can be a tricky proposition, especially in the crowded start-up market.

People often ask how I built up BodeTree's media presence over the past few years. After all, we're still a relatively small company focused on the unsexy small business space. We don't have a dedicated media team, and we're located in Denver instead of in a media hub like New York or San Francisco. Still, we've managed to gain coverage in big-name publications.

Over the years, our media presence has proven to be one our most cost-effective and important marketing channels. We have also learned a few tricks that help us garner media coverage without breaking the bank with a regular PR firm retainer.

MAKE A POWERFUL GRAB FOR ATTENTION

There's no magic formula for becoming an attention magnet. It all comes down to your personal style and relationship with reporters. The trick is to think creatively about what you're willing to do for attention.

Take Lady Gaga, for example. Up until a few years ago, she was a rather ordinary struggling singer-songwriter. However, she had a huge amount of personal drive and was brave enough to create an outrageous public image that defined her.

Fortunately, gaining media attention does not require that you be an inherently theatrical person. Creating an "outrageous" public persona can mean simply thinking outside the box for your given industry.

My company, BodeTree, for example, approaches small-business financial management in a striking way—we're inspired by the Buddhist legend of the Bodhi Tree, under which Buddha reached the highest state of enlightenment, and we believe that financial enlightenment can be similarly reached. I can say with some certainty that we are the only financial company to cite Buddhist legend in their mission. However, our unconventional approach sets us apart and makes our story more appealing in the media and with potential clients and partners.

BECOME AN INCREDIBLE SOURCE

I started to build my media relationships by offering support to journalists whom I respected. I read through my target publication or watched a television show religiously to see whose writing and reporting seemed most closely to match my own interests. Then I sent that person ideas, content, and support.

The important lesson I learned was to avoid outright self-promotion. Instead, I focused on helping journalists find background information, identify trends, or provide a new take on something they had already produced. I also reached out to ask for advice and more information about things they had already written.

As long as you are honest and authentic in your approach, your interest and support will be well received. Once you establish a relationship, you can come back with a pitch to them along with feedback on the help they provided.

WRITE YOUR OWN STORY

Developing content for media partners helps position yourself and your company as an expert in a particular area. If you are successful in getting your company's story out to the media, you'll eventually run out of things to discuss. After all, a product launch is only relevant right when it's happening. Inevitably, you'll have to start creating content that doesn't directly focus on your product or company.

Be open to new ways of sharing your company story through blogs, social media, and video. Use catchy phrases and hashtags to set your story apart or take advantage of trends.

Try to become a storyteller for your audience, drawing on analogies with which they are already familiar. Don't be afraid to use classic story plots or myth references. Storylines that people can recognize right away have the power of allowing them to follow where you're leading them, and reporters can easily pick up on that.

BE RELENTLESS

This is by far the most important tip I have to offer. I can guarantee that you will experience a lot of rejection when it comes to building a media presence. Get used to the standard response of, "Thanks, but I'll pass," or to even no response at all. Don't give up. Be patient and polite, listening to their responses and criticisms and trying to answer them—and always try to help them see that they need what you've got.

Just remember that media is not a one-size-fits-all prospect. Each writer has a distinctive voice and an editor or boss who has clearly defined priorities, and those needs and priorities are constantly shifting. Recognize that a news event can change the game in a flash. If you can trim your sails to catch those changes in the news cycle and avoid the slow spots that inevitably develop in that same cycle, you can keep coming back until you hit the mark.

Think of yourself as a missionary—once your message is heard, it has the power to change people's lives. Regardless of how firmly you believe that, you must approach the media with that sense of messianic mission, and the passion will come through.

MANAGING YOUR MARKETING SPEND

Of all the decisions that entrepreneurs face, deciding when to start invest-ing in marketing is one of the most difficult. If you ramp up your marketing spending too early in your life cycle, you run the risk of burning cash with very little to show for it. On the other hand, if you wait too long to get serious about marketing, you risk being eclipsed by the competition and never reaching the scale you desire.

The abstract nature of marketing and the uncertainty that goes along with launching a new initiative is enough to drive a founder to the brink. Fortunately, the decision process doesn't have to be as painful as we often perceive it to be. In fact, I've found that there are only three major con-cepts that you need to master before making your marketing move.

HAVE YOU FOUND PRODUCT/MARKET FIT?

This is the single most important factor for any business, regardless of size or industry. The good news is that you don't have to spend heavily on marketing to prove to the world that the product you have built serves the market you want to serve.

At BodeTree, we took to the streets of our local community to con-nect with small-business owners and learn about their unique needs. From there, we revised both our product and our message to reflect what we learned from our prospective customers.

We held back from spending on marketing until we were confident that we had the right fit. This decision was often easier said than done, mostly because it takes a lot of time to reach product/market fit, and the temptation just to dive in and push for growth can be strong. However, the disciplined approach that we adopted ensured that we didn't burn through cash too early and helped us create a solid foundation for the future.

DO YOU UNDERSTAND YOUR CUSTOMER-ACQUISITION COST?

For those who aren't familiar with this concept, customer-acquisition cost (CAC) is the average cost of attracting a new user or customer to your business. For many companies, CAC is the single most important cost in the business. Marketing, of course, is the "cost" part of customer-acquisition cost.

Depending on how much and how often your customers spend with you, it's entirely possible that the cost to bring in a new customer could exceed the revenue generated by that customer. In other words, if your acquisition cost isn't well managed or focused exclusively on getting in front of potential customers, it's possible you'll find yourself quickly going broke.

CAN YOU SUPPORT NEW CUSTOMERS?

Last, but not least, entrepreneurs have to make sure that their organizations are prepared to support the marketing initiative and the growth that will result from it. Far too often, founders focus so much on product and strategy that they neglect to develop strong service and support teams internally. If the growth you've been chasing arrives ahead of your ability to support it, you might not get the chance to catch up. Remember—one bad customer experience can poison a client forever.

With BodeTree, we were lucky that we built out a customer support channel early on in our history as a direct result of our efforts to find product/market fit. We took an extremely hands-on approach when it came to learning what customers cared about, and eventually that communication style simply became part of our company's culture. Once we felt prepared to increase our marketing spend, we were confident that we had the right internal processes in place to support the new growth.

The decision to ramp up marketing spend has the potential to make or break any organization. While every business is different, there are core concepts that always hold true. Every single entrepreneur, regardless of industry, size, or sophistication, needs to understand product/market fit, customer-acquisition cost, and customer service before spending heavily on marketing. Only then can you ensure that the effort and resources you put toward marketing your product or service will pay off.

WRITE EVERY SINGLE DAY

One benefit of starting a company is that you get to meet a lot of interesting people. If you're smart, you make the most of this benefit by asking them for advice. I've found that most people jump at the chance to share their knowledge and wisdom. Sometimes even the most casual exchanges can lead to life-changing realizations.

The best advice I ever received came from Ellen McGirt, one of my favorite journalists. I'm almost positive that she doesn't remember me (or the advice she gave, for that matter), but her insight had a tremendous effect on my life.

I met Ellen at a dinner party hosted by *Fast Company* magazine back in late 2012. I have no idea how I ended up getting an invite, but I jumped at the opportunity to attend. Ellen was incredibly friendly and generous with her time. When I asked her for advice, she didn't hesitate. She told me to keep a journal about my experiences starting BodeTree and to write every day without fail.

It didn't matter how much I wrote or how good my writing was; the only thing that mattered was that I put words to paper without fail. I took her advice to heart and soon found that the act of writing every day had a transformative effect on my life and my business.

WRITING IS THERAPEUTIC

Entrepreneurship can be a stressful, terrifying, and lonely journey. Even for individuals who have great support networks and cofounders, it can still be difficult to find an outlet through which to vent. After all, spouses can get concerned about how your challenges will affect their lives, and fellow entrepreneurs are often too wrapped up in their own difficulties to listen to yours.

Writing, however, is the perfect outlet for explaining, exploring, and digesting everything that you face as an entrepreneur. I've found that after I write, my challenges seem smaller, and the future looks brighter. It's only when I trap negative thoughts in my mind that they fester into anxiety and depression.

WRITING PROMOTES INTROSPECTION

Far too many people are oblivious to their shortcomings. Perhaps we're conditioned by society to ignore any negative aspects of ourselves, or maybe people just don't take time for deep introspection anymore. Regardless, I've found that the act of writing forces me to be introspective. I know that my writing has helped me in identifying my weaknesses, understanding them, and learning how they affect those around me.

The act of articulating and sharing my personal shortcomings in a public forum has become a way for me to gain control over them. For example, I've struggled in the past when it came to dealing with uncertainty and the anxiety that goes along with it. It was only after reflecting on these challenges through writing that I realized how to embrace those challenges in order to find the strength to move forward. The resulting shift in my perspective has been life changing. That's why I encourage every entrepreneur I meet to take time for daily introspective writing. It not only makes you a better leader but can also make you a better person.

WRITING TRAINS YOUR MIND TO THINK CLEARLY

Writing is a lot like exercise: the more you do it, the easier it becomes. When writing about a topic, you have to wrestle with it in your mind, forcing you to identify key points and arrive at conclusions.

This increase in mental clarity has been the most important benefit I've taken away from my writing. It has helped me develop the ability to absorb quickly the most important aspects of a given situation, synthesizing them into a narrative and drawing a well-supported conclusion. This has become an invaluable skill for me as a leader, because it increases confidence in my decision-making process. It isn't a skill that can be acquired overnight. Rather, it's one that must be nurtured over time through disciplined daily writing.

I will be forever grateful to Ellen for the phenomenal advice she gave me. The benefits that I've accrued from writing every day are too great to quantify. It has become part of my routine—equal parts therapy, introspection, and mental exercise. That's why I make an effort to offer the same advice to other entrepreneurs I encounter. Who knows? Perhaps someday I'll have a similar effect on the life of someone I encounter at a dinner party.

LEARN TO MAKE A LASTING IMPRESSION

There are two types of entrepreneurs in this world: those who have the natural ability to connect with people and those who don't. Unfortunately, I fall into the latter category. I've always been deeply envious of individuals who demonstrate that relaxed and natural magnetism that both attracts and engages on a deeply personal level. What sets them apart from the rest of us, and how can we learn from them to become better communicators? The answer came to me while attending a trade show.

Over the course of the event, I watched a lot of sales pitches, both good and bad, and came to a key realization: Maya Angelou was right—people don't remember what you said, but they absolutely remember how you made them feel. The people who I once thought were simply naturally good communicators know this and use it to their advantage. Here's how the rest of us can learn from them.

BE EMPATHETIC

Effective and persuasive communication starts with empathy. The best vendors at the trade show were able to draw people in and get them talking. They didn't try to push their agenda on the people who stopped by their booth. Instead, they were able to connect with them on a personal level and get the other person to share their pain. From there, the vendors were able to capitalize on that pain and offer relevant solutions to the prospect's problems. They were able to empathize with their prospect's hopes, dreams, and fears and in doing so were able to change the dynamic of the entire interaction. It was no longer a matter of selling a product or service. Instead, it was a matter of helping the other person out, and this made a world of difference.

BE PROVOCATIVE

Not everyone is self-aware enough to know that he or she is experiencing pain. After all, it's easy to become so used to a bad situation that you simply accept it as something that cannot be changed. At the bank-technology trade show I attended, many of the financial institutions in attendance demonstrated this behavior. It proved to be a challenge for some of the most innovative vendors who were trying to solve those pervasive and difficult problems. The less effective communicators did their best to explain the nature of the problem that the banker was experiencing and then position their product as the solution. More often than not, this failed to resonate, because the banker had become used to the problem and didn't feel the need to change.

The best communicators, however, were provocative and planted the seed of doubt in the minds of their prospects. They were able to ask the tough questions and create enough interest that the bankers they were dealing with started to question their long-held beliefs. It wasn't a matter of being alarmist or inflammatory. They simply were able to get people thinking and create momentum for their cause.

Be Authentic

Perhaps the most important observation was that nothing is as important as authenticity. People may not be self-aware, but they can spot a phony from a mile away. One of the keynote speakers at the event was Guy Kawasaki, the famed tech evangelist and thought leader. Guy explored the science behind authenticity, explaining how certain incredibly subtle facial expressions could indicate whether someone had an authentic smile. It was an amazing observation that I saw play out in real time.

The smarmy, inauthentic vendors struggled to retain the attention of their prospects even when they had a compelling product. The people who were authentic in their interactions, however, fared much better. It seemed as though prospective customers cared far more about the vendors' authenticity than about the features and functions of the products they were selling.

The single most important thing I've come to realize is that emotion trumps logic every time. It's what drives people to take action. Even the most articulate and factual argument will fall on deaf ears if it doesn't elicit an emotional response. There's no magic formula for connecting with people on the emotional plane, but if you're empathetic, provocative, and authentic in your interactions, you won't go wrong. You'll be on the path to becoming an incredibly effective communicator. After all, people won't remember what you said, but they will absolutely remember how you made them feel.

GAINING TRACTION

THE THREE WORST NEGOTIATION MISTAKES YOU CAN MAKE

When you're an entrepreneur, almost everything is a negotiation. You negotiate with everyone from clients to partners—and sometimes even employees. Negotiation is a fundamental part of the entrepreneurial experience. Unfortunately, many entrepreneurs fall victim to mistakes that make them incredibly poor negotiators.

Over my past five years as CEO, I've not only witnessed these mistakes play out but also made a number of them myself. Fortunately, it's never too late to identify these mistakes and change direction. Here are the top three reasons why you're failing as a negotiator—and how to overcome them.

YOU'RE GREEDY

Nothing can derail a negotiation more quickly than greed. If one party pushes for too much or is too aggressive, the relationships between those involved grow sour, and the negotiation can go south. I'm a diehard skeptic about the claim that "this isn't personal—it's strictly business." All business is personal, and emotions run high. It's only natural for people to overestimate the value of their product, position, or contribution in a negotiation. It takes a special skill to recognize greedy behavior and stop it before it gets out of control.

This style of negotiation can be difficult to master, because no matter how hard you try, emotions inevitably influence your actions. The temptation to squeeze a partner for a better deal or emerge "victorious" in the negotiation can be strong, and it takes a solid sense of self-awareness and humility to resist.

YOU DON'T UNDERSTAND THE TYPE OF NEGOTIATION YOU'RE CONDUCTING

Leaders frequently encounter two types of negotiations. The first is what I describe as the asset negotiation, which is generally a one-time event resulting in clear winners and losers. A good example of this type of negotiation is the sale of an asset, such as a piece of equipment.

In this situation, the seller wants to maximize the price paid at all costs and doesn't really care about the long-term implications of the deal. After all, once the deal is done, the seller generally won't have to work with the buyer again. The negotiators are incentivized to view the situation as a zero-sum game in which someone wins and someone loses, which naturally leads to a more aggressive exchange.

The second type of negotiation—when both parties involved have to maintain a working relationship long after the negotiation ends—is more complex and thus involves a more sophisticated approach. It's important to remember that intangibles, such as trust, respect, and admiration, have tremendous value in business and must be factored into the negotiation strategy and defended at all costs.

You Gamble with Things You Can't Afford to Lose

When you play hardball with another party, you must always recognize that your counterpart can simply walk away. This can be tricky when it comes to strategic relationships, because there's often significant cost and pain associated with a potential dissolution.

However, there is a point in most negotiations beyond which the pain of dissolution is preferable to an inequitable outcome. If a relationship is truly central to your success as an organization, you must temper your desire to play hardball or else risk losing everything.

When it comes to negotiation, entrepreneurs are often their own worst enemies. Ego-driven mistakes take their toll and make the process more painful than it has to be. Remember that successful negotiations require three things.

First, there is simply no room for greedy behavior in successful negotiations. Second, both parties must recognize the nature of the negotiation itself—if, going forward, you have to work together, the negotiation cannot be a zero-sum game. And finally, maintaining perspective on what you are and aren't willing to part with in the negotiation is invaluable. All too often people get too comfortable in a relationship and overplay their hand in negotiations. When this happens, they run the risk of losing everything, and that is the worst outcome of all.

TRUE GRIT

Business is a game of dramatic ups and downs, especially for teams that are trying to create something new or bring about meaningful change in a stagnant and complacent market. It's easy to feel a bit bipolar at times. Some days you're on top of the world, but other days you're just trying to stay alive. How a team manages these swings, and the periods of adversity in particular, is what separates successful businesses from failures.

Every business encounters adversity. It's one of the few constants that you can count on and it can be all too easy to allow these setbacks to get you down, discourage your efforts, and extinguish the fire that keeps you going. Good leaders recognize this fact but find the courage and wherewithal to help their teams avoid these pitfalls.

I'm not an expert on many things, but one area in which I have plenty of experience is dealing with adversity. At BodeTree, my team and I have had our fair share of failures, strikeouts, and unfair situations. Despite these setbacks, however, we always keep moving forward. We've learned to use adversity to our advantage, and it all comes down to one trait: grit.

REMEMBER THAT CHARACTER IS KING

Grit is just another word for strength of character. An individual or team who displays grit is someone who can take a hit and just keep on going, no matter what. This resilience enables successful teams to avoid the pitfalls of depression, lethargy, and apathy that people tend to run into when faced with adversity. It may seem like grit is an innate virtue that people are either born with or not, but this isn't the case. Grit can be developed, just like any other skill.

Developing grit in yourself is difficult; trying to develop it in others is even harder. It takes equal parts understanding, compassion, and dedication. Over the years at BodeTree, I've learned that grit starts with intellectual honesty and the ability to face your fears. Leaders looking to foster gritty teams can start by fostering an environment of transparency and trust.

When team members know how they're being judged and what the expectations are, they're more willing to be honest about shortcomings and face their fears. If team members feel as though their next mistake will be their last, anxiety sets in—and people tend to crumble in the face of adversity. Leaders must create an environment that encourages grit and resilient thinking across the board.

Turn Anger and Frustration into Something Productive

If you've developed a gritty team, you can use adversity and challenges to your advantage. There are only two ways to handle bad situations: you can accept what happened and roll over, or you can get mad. I've found that turning the other cheek is rarely productive in business. Instead, I like to work to focus the collective anger and frustration of my team into something productive and transformational.

We've faced some difficult situations at BodeTree over the last few years, including deals and partnerships falling through at the eleventh hour. The news can be devastating at first, but it can also be motivating. We've learned to let our feelings of self-pity give way to righteous indignation. We channel our anger into productivity and let it renew our passion to bring about change. For us, succeeding in our space is no longer a matter of business or strategy; it's personal.

I'm fortunate to have such a dedicated and gritty team. The adversity we've faced could have derailed us, robbed us of our drive, and dampened our will to move forward. Lesser teams would have crumbled, but we've managed to turn adversity into an advantage. Our anger and resilience pushes us forward and gives us purpose. We've become a team hell-bent on constantly advancing, uninterested in anything short of total market dominance.

I hope that our experience can serve as an example for other teams. You will face adversity in your endeavors no matter what they are—that much is certain. Just remember that success isn't determined by whether you encounter challenges but rather by the way you respond to those challenges. Leaders of teams must work to develop grit, both in them-selves and in the people they lead.

The resilience that results will enable individuals and teams to trans-form anger and frustration into a powerful motivator that can spur you onward even in the most difficult of circumstances.

Finding Balance in Big Data

One of my favorite quotes comes from W. Edwards Deming: "In God we trust. All others must bring data." Demings, a management consultant, helped Japanese industry get back on its feet in the aftermath of World War II by introducing a revolutionary data-driven approach to business. His words always make me chuckle, because they perfectly encapsulate what I deal with on a near-daily basis at BodeTree.

I've found that when it comes to partnerships and business development opportunities, everyone wants to derisk situations to the best of their abilities. More often than not, that means building a comprehensive business case with data to back up all the assumptions about how the business will perform.

Over the past five years, I've been on both sides of the data equation. Throughout my journey, my views on the role of data inside of an organization have evolved, and I've learned to embrace a balanced approach to data-driven decision making that honors both the qualitative and quantitative aspects of the business.

Data as a Crutch

When we first launched the company back in 2010, all our prospective partners wanted hard data to help them make a decision about whether to proceed with us. They wanted to know exactly how the product would be received by potential users, how it would be used, and how much revenue the partnership would generate for their company.

All these were valid questions, but at the time, we simply didn't know the answers. We were early on in the process and hadn't been able to prove out our assumptions at scale. It was a frustrating time for our team—how could we get the data we needed to prove out our premise if no one gave us a chance?

This catch-22 scenario led me to develop a certain bitterness toward the concept of big data. For me, reliance on data alone was little more than a crutch for individuals who lacked vision. We were forced to slog it out on our own for a time, winning small battles here and there but ultimately doing whatever we could to win over users. It was only after we managed to collect a meaningful set of data that I began to understand data's importance.

Many of our original assumptions proved to be inaccurate, and we would never have recognized that if we hadn't analyzed the data. As it turns out, data wasn't a crutch—it was a vital part of the overall planning process. My frustration was not with the people asking for data but with my inability to produce that data as early or easily as I wanted.

INNOVATION MEANS ACCEPTING UNCERTAINTY

Still, if you're building an innovative, strategically differentiated product or company, you won't have enough data to derisk the entire concept for partners early on. That's when I think an overreliance on data can be problematic. Many of our partners want the best of both worlds: seeking innovation and strategic differentiation while having absolute certainty about how it will work out. Unfortunately, those two things are mutually exclusive.

After running into this conundrum repeatedly, we came to learn that intuition was sometimes the most important driver for strategically important decisions. Big data cannot replace intuition; instead, it exists to complement it and hold it accountable to reality. It can be relied on to make highly necessary, tactical decisions to help you realize your long-term vision, but it should never be allowed to stand in the way of innovation. If you're seeking certainty in every decision you make, you'll almost always miss out on transformative opportunities.

FINDING A BALANCED APPROACH

Balance seems to be an ongoing theme of mine lately, perhaps because there are few things in life as important as seeking balance. Today's world is full of binaries—in politics, you are either right or left, and in business, you are either a data fanatic or an intuitive decision maker—and now few gray areas remain.

However, when we step back and rethink our challenges through a balanced lens, the solutions become instantly clear. Combining entrepreneurial intuition with concrete data analysis can propel businesses forward while grounding progress in reality. In short, I've learned that leaders should not look to data alone for answers but should instead use it to broaden their perspective and challenge previously held beliefs.

EMBRACING THE AGONY OF FAILURE

Entrepreneurs tend to have a complicated relationship with failure. On one hand, it's a necessary part of the creation process. Innovation of any kind is usually a direct result of multiple failed attempts. On the other hand, the thought of failure is something that can influence your decisions, bring you heartache, and keep you up at night.

In any endeavor, failure of some kind is inevitable. Everyone will experience it in one form or another, but when dealt with productively, failure can propel an entrepreneur to unexpected levels of success.

START WITH SELF-AWARENESS

As with most things in life, honesty comes first. Failures can come in all shapes and sizes, and it's easy to gloss over or downplay the small losses as a daily part of life. I'll admit that I'm guilty of this myself.

Early on at BodeTree, we built a product we were proud of and that we felt served the needs of small-business owners. We received positive reviews and media coverage, and we even managed to sign several large partnership agreements. The only problem with our story was that after they signed up, a huge number of users failed to progress through the system we designed. We were perplexed. After all, the setup process was intuitive and fairly quick. All they had to do was sync with their QuickBooks system, and then they would be ready to go. We knew there were about six million QuickBooks users in the United States, so why were so few taking advantage of our solution?

What became clear to us was that far fewer than six million people used QuickBooks on a regular basis. Intuit's figures were technically accurate, but they reflected people who used any part of QuickBooks, not just the bookkeeping features. We called this realization "The 90 Percent Challenge," and it became a central tenet of our company.

This revelation meant that we had made a big bet based on the wrong information. We depended on the false reality that people had solid accounting systems—that they actually used—in order for our product to work. Our entire business model had been built on it.

Overnight, we were forced to acknowledge that our addressable market was less than a sixth of what we thought it was. For my team members, the temptation to fall into despair or desperately cling to earlier assumptions was strong. Ultimately, I knew we had to accept reality for what it was and live to fight another day. Once we were honest with ourselves about the problem, we could turn our focus toward solving it.

ACCEPT REALITY AND ADJUST ACCORDINGLY

Once you've come to terms with your failures, the next step is to adjust accordingly. At BodeTree, we knew that our market was still small businesses and that our earlier QuickBooks-centric model wouldn't work at scale. We decided to remove our dependence on QuickBooks by connecting directly to financial institutions to get our data. As a result, our addressable market went from fewer than one million small businesses to about thirty million overnight.

Our massive new market opportunity, however, did not come without another set of challenges. To connect to this pool of potential small-business customers, we would need to ask for online banking logins, which, despite our rock-solid security, would inevitably cause some hesitation. Even worse, the development work required to make this happen would cost upward of $100,000. While we had cash in the bank, any significant spending is cause for concern when you're a start-up. Despite the challenges, we knew what we needed to do, and we opted to move forward.

I knew that the entire organization had to rally around this adjustment if we were going to be successful. To accomplish this, I made sure that every key stakeholder had input into the decision process. In doing so, I removed the potential for dissent and second-guessing after we started development. We moved swiftly to rebuild the core elements of the system and fix the recognized problems.

KEEP MOVING FORWARD

The absolute worst thing you can do when you encounter failure is to let it get in your head. The creeping doubts, insecurities, and negativity that often accompany failures big and small can act like a cancer in your organization, sapping your energy and destroying your momentum.

So much of business comes down to psychological momentum, which is defined as a state of mind in which individuals or team members feel that things are going unstoppably their way. It's a well-known concept in the world of sports. According to the American Psychological Association's Review of General Psychology, 92 percent of football coaches believe their performance is "crucially determined by momentum." Initial success frequently leads to more success; conversely, failure tends to lead to more failure.

That's why it is so important to acknowledge failure, adjust accordingly, and move on. Dwelling on the past and letting it influence the future is a recipe for disaster. Learn from your shortcomings, and always keep moving forward. If you can deal with life's inevitable failures more effectively, you may start to find that they can become stepping-stones to greatness.

A BUSINESS IN MOTION TENDS TO STAY IN MOTION

The effects of momentum on a team's performance are one of the most interesting yet intuitive elements in business. Often intangible, nothing has a greater effect on the morale and performance of an organization than the perception of momentum—or the lack thereof. Its presence can be felt on every level, subtly driving people to accomplish great things. The trouble with momentum, of course, is that once you lose it, it's difficult to get moving again.

I'm fond of saying that BodeTree was a five-year overnight success. It's easy to look at our success and think that we found a winning formula in a short time. In reality, it took many years of hard work and a lot of dead ends to get to where we are today. Once we finally managed to build momentum in the marketplace, we had to learn quickly how to keep it going and turn it into a long-term sustainable advantage. After all, "objects in motion tend to stay in motion."

FOCUS ON EXECUTION

Nothing kills momentum more quickly than poor execution does. As a young organization, it's easy to focus on chasing opportunities rather than building out the internal resources needed to execute on those opportunities. When this happens, companies tend to stumble out of the gate rather than executing on their objectives efficiently and effectively.

Failure to execute can destroy forward momentum in two ways. First, it damages both your relationships with clients and your reputation in the marketplace. Second, and perhaps more important, poor execution undermines the confidence of your team. People begin to question everything from product quality to their abilities. This vicious cycle leads to even worse execution going forward.

At BodeTree, my team and I manage to prevent this through a maniacal focus on execution. This can be a particularly difficult balancing act as it means pushing both sides of the sales and execution teams out of their comfort zones.

The sales team is forced to operate within the constraints of the organization's competencies and resources, and the execution team is often forced to get creative to serve the needs of the customer. Ultimately, solid execution leads to happy customers, and happy customers lead to increased sales. In the end, continued success comes down to our ability to execute as well as generate prospects.

KEEP BUILDING YOUR PIPELINE
It's equally important for sales teams to be constantly searching for new opportunities, even when attention has been shifted inward toward execution. It's easy for sales teams to unintentionally take on account management functions as clients move to the execution phase. The reason for this is simple—sales professionals invest their blood, sweat, and tears into building client relationships, and that makes it difficult for them to let go.

However, if the sales team shifts their focus from finding new deals, even for a moment, the effect can ripple throughout the organization. Although the lack of pipeline may go unnoticed in the near term, eventually the lack of new prospects will have a stifling effect on the organization.

My team and I managed to avoid this pipeline process by adopting a hybrid approach to account management. When a new client signs a contract, our sales team retains primary ownership of that relationship. However, they bring in support from our marketing and support teams so that they don't have to focus on day-to-day operations. Instead, they're free to prospect for new opportunities in the market and keep our pipeline strong.

ALWAYS THINK AHEAD
Managing forward momentum requires leaders always to think three or four steps ahead of where they are today. While technology can scale quickly, human capital does not. The support infrastructure that is necessary to serve an influx of clients takes time to develop. Again, leaders have to find balance when it comes to staffing up and managing demand. Hire

too early and you burn cash while employees sit idle; hire too late and you're always behind the curve.

In the past, my team and I were too conservative when it came to hiring additional resources. We tended to wait until a deal was closed before hiring new people. While this saved capital, it also meant that we had to train staff in the middle of a deployment. After learning the hard way, we adopted a new model that proved to be significantly more effective.

We now measure our team resources against the anticipated demand that a new deal will bring. If we determine that additional resources will be needed, we start the hiring process as soon as we enter into the contract negotiation phase with our clients. This ensures that our new team members are fully trained and up to speed well in advance.

Momentum is a precious resource in business. It invigorates the team and opens up new and exciting opportunities. However, failure to execute, staff appropriately, or maintain the pipeline can stop momentum in its tracks. The trick to maintaining momentum is to find balance. It isn't easy to juggle sales, execution, and staffing, but if you can manage it, you'll find that short-term momentum will translate into a sustainable advantage for years to come.

WINNING ONE INCH AT A TIME

Life at a start-up is anything but boring. Regardless of your role, you're always working on new deals, exploring interesting new opportunities, and planning for the next phase of growth. It is easy to get caught up in the hustle and lose perspective when you're so busy, so when you're in the thick of it, try to take some time off to reflect on everything that has been happening.

Once, during my time away from the office, I rewatched the 1999 film *Any Given Sunday* and was struck by the rousing speech the main character gave toward the end of the movie. In it, the head coach of a fictional football team tells his players that life is a game of inches. The only way to move forward is to fight, tooth and nail, for every inch of ground. At the end of the day, the total of those inches separates the winners from the losers. Running a business is no different.

Most successful businesses are defined by the sum of all of the little decisions and interactions that happen every day, not by grand strategic moves. This simple truth puts the responsibility on both leaders and teams to make every single moment count.

BUSINESSES WIN ONE INCH AT A TIME

If you look back on past jobs or relationships, it's usually hard to pinpoint a specific event that made that experience good or bad. Rather, the totality of all the interactions influences your perception. The same can be said of running your own business.

Most businesses grow through the steady march of small wins rather than one or two major home runs. This can seem tedious at times, but recognizing that entrepreneurship is a game of inches is vital to success. Each day, entrepreneurs, leaders, and team members have to find the will to work (and sometimes fight) for the next inch of progress. It is in this struggle that successful businesses are forged.

This is something we've struggled with at BodeTree. We sell primarily to banks and other traditional organizations, so our sales cycle tends to be on the long side. Weeks will go by during which we don't see major movement in some of the deals we're working on; rather, we inch forward, slowly but surely. At times, it has been excruciating, but now that I look back I can see that those little wins created a strong foundation for the business. It's important for leaders to recognize this and reinforce the value of these little wins to the entire team.

You Either Win as a Team or Lose Alone

These little wins are only possible when you have a team that is aligned, both culturally and intellectually. When you're pushing forward with a plan, it's all too easy to let your personal goals and ambitions get in the way of what is best for the team. Sometimes it's a short-term focus on hitting a bonus target; other times it's the temptation to do what is best for you as a founder.

It doesn't matter what form it takes. Whenever we put ourselves ahead of the team, the business suffers. You either win as a team or die as individuals, and only an honest, aligned, and fully attuned team has any hope of winning a game of inches.

At BodeTree, we've been lucky to have a strong core team from day one. However, this doesn't mean that we're always perfect. As with any team, we have to contend with the temptation to put your personal interests ahead of those of the organization. This usually means that team members (myself included) tend to favor our areas of focus, be it product development, strategy, or sales. It's a perfectly natural occurrence, but one that cannot be allowed to thrive. That's why my team and I encourage frank and open discussion about decisions that are being made. While this process isn't always elegant, it does ensure that we move forward as a team, not as a collection of individuals who have differing agendas.

Taking the Easy Way Out Rarely Pays Off

I've learned that it is important for leaders and their teams to stay committed to the long-haul approach and avoid chasing too many shortcuts. Growth accelerators and big wins aren't a bad thing by any measure, but when an organization tries to jump from moonshot to moonshot, it tends to be damaging.

Everybody wants to find quick and easy wins, but those are few and far between. The never-ending roller coaster of emotional highs and lows crushes morale and leads to short-term decision making.

There's no doubt about it: creating, running, and growing a business is hard. It's the ability to keep moving forward, inch by inch, that separates the winners from the losers. More important, it's the ability to remain positive and aligned while gaining those inches that separates good companies from great ones.

There's No Such Thing as Magic

I've found that in business, coming up with new ideas and identifying exciting opportunities is easy. Executing on those ideas, however, is incredibly difficult. Execution takes time, dedication, and a lot of hard work. It's an unglamorous but entirely necessary process.

Unfortunately, many entrepreneurs become blinded to the details of execution whenever an exciting idea or opportunity arises. They demonstrate a tendency to jump ahead of the rest of the team, overlooking the tactical steps that everyone must take in order to turn a dream into a reality.

They just want things to work, and they act as though the nuance and detail of execution will magically take care of themselves. It's important for leaders to recognize this tendency and bridge the gap between ideas and execution. After all, when it comes to business, there is no such thing as magic.

Plan for Execution from the Beginning

At BodeTree, partnerships are at the very core of our strategy. As a result, we spend the vast majority of our time nurturing relationships and working toward successful partner implementations. Early on, I had the tendency to get ahead of myself when it came to these partnerships. More often than not, I saw the synergies that could exist between our companies and conveniently skipped past some of the logistical issues that had to take place to make them a reality. I was so blinded by the allure of the deal that I overlooked glaring red flags on the path to execution.

Whether a matter of technical integration or product functionality that simply didn't exist, I operated under the assumption that we'd deal with issues when the time came. The result of this flawed thinking was that opportunities had a tendency to go sideways over time. When it came time to execute, the concessions we had to make changed the fundamental nature of the opportunity. I quickly learned the value of solid execution and the need to consider tactics right from the start.

We adopted the mantra "work with what you have" internally, and we began to consider the reality of our product and team's constraints earlier on in the process. Because we were able to deliver value sooner and more efficiently, this led to more successful partnerships.

DON'T EXPECT OTHERS TO SHARE YOUR VISION

Successful execution depends greatly on whether every person involved in the process has an aligned vision of success. In the past, I've been guilty of simply assuming that my team and partners share my vision of how the opportunity in question will play out. The reality, however, is that people's visions and perceptions rarely align on their own. Everyone connects the dots differently and draws unique conclusions. Although this can lead to cohesive, well-rounded solutions, more often than not, this misalignment leads to confusion and poor execution.

Over the years, I've realized that leaders have to put a lot of work into aligning people's understandings, perceptions, and visions of success. As a result, my team and I have perfected the art of overcommunication. We've found that you have to go out of your way to align the team's understanding and commitment throughout the entire execution process. Weekly check-in meetings, personal conversations, and group alignment sessions go a long way toward supporting successful execution.

REMEMBER THAT PEOPLE TAKE THE PATH OF LEAST RESISTANCE

One of the most significant mistakes I made early on was ignoring the fact that people take the path of least resistance. When my team and I approached an exciting opportunity, we assumed that our potential partners were just as excited.

This led to frustration when our counterparts ended up taking the more expedient route when faced with challenges. Our execution plans assumed that people would behave in a certain way because we assumed they'd see the benefits as we did, despite the extra effort it involved.. When we ran into difficulties, we tried to change their behavior rather than adjusting our plans. Perhaps not surprisingly, this attempt failed time after time.

I eventually realized that we'd never be able to change people's behaviors. Rather, the team and I had to recognize their path of least resistance and adjust our execution plan accordingly. Once we started to tailor our approach to our partners and stopped trying to change their behavior, everything became easier. Whenever we encountered a roadblock, we were able to pivot our approach and work within our partners' constraints to accomplish our goals.

Nothing in business comes easy; anything that is worthwhile takes work. It's easy, as an entrepreneur, to become blind to the realities of execution and to hope that things will always work out just as we envision they will. As a leader, I've learned to avoid this pitfall and focus on the nuance of execution at all stages of the game. If you don't, it's unlikely that your dreams will become a reality.

FINDING PRODUCT/MARKET FIT

When it comes to starting a business, finding product/market fit is the only thing that matters. I've met some smart entrepreneurs who built a great product but who then ultimately found that consumer demand was lower than expected. It is incredibly easy to get so wrapped up in creating something that you fail to stop and consider whether there's a receptive market for it.

It's a situation that I found myself in shortly after launching my business in 2011. We had what I thought was a great product, but we simply didn't see the flood of users we expected. Rather than give up, however, we overcame this challenge by thinking critically about our position in the market and adopting these three strategies.

EXPAND YOUR MARKET

When we launched BodeTree, we placed a major bet on one of our main partner's app center. With millions of small businesses making up their base, it was the perfect channel for us—or so we thought. Shortly after we went live, we started to see that there weren't nearly as many small businesses visiting the app center as we had originally expected.

Additionally, we discovered that accountants and other advisers made up a sizeable portion of the overall traffic, which was a major hurdle for us because we had designed our product only for small-business owners.

To solve for this, we opted to expand our market. First, we found ways to expand beyond that single partner and their app center. We've partnered with innovative, up-and-coming companies in the same space and formed relationships with small-business aggregators. Second, we expanded our product to fit the market we had, not the market we wanted.

My team fundamentally rethought our approach, choosing to connect directly to clients' source data rather than via accounting systems. It expanded our addressable market from about one million small businesses to about thirty million. Ultimately, we were able to take decisive action that helped us expand our addressable market and drive better adoption of our product.

FIND THE RIGHT PRODUCT HOOK

Some products offer customers instant gratification (such as retail websites), whereas others fall into the "slow burn" category and offer delayed satisfaction (like a gym membership). Unfortunately, BodeTree fell into the latter category, and that made it difficult for us to scale as quickly as we wanted. To solve this, we set out to develop a multipronged approach that helped us hook users early on and then gradually introduce them to the other longer-term elements of the product.

We launched our funding center, which used the data we have in our system, to help our users connect with capital faster than ever before. The act of helping them secure funding solved an immediate need for our customers while also leading them to take advantage of our other features. In short, we found ways to create the right features and offers that spoke to our users' immediate needs and then guided them to take advantage of the rest of the system.

MAKE SURE YOU'RE SERVING THE RIGHT CUSTOMERS

Finally, we took a moment to step back and determine whether we were serving the right customer in the first place. After all, even if you can expand your market and hook users early, you can still run into problems if the avenues where you connect with those users aren't efficient. Finding and connecting with small-business owners is like hand-to-hand combat—dangerous and draining. We knew we had to make sure not only that we found the right channels but also that we were serving the right customer.

We eventually came to the realization that our best customers were the organizations that aggregate, connect, and serve small businesses rather than the small businesses themselves. By selling to these organizations and helping them add more value to their existing customer base, we could connect with small businesses more efficiently than by relying on direct outreach alone.

Ultimately, we managed to expand the business by serving these ideal customers while continuing to serve our original base of small businesses.

This decision has led to a dramatic increase in our customer count and a new period of success.

The principles I have learned at BodeTree can be applied to any new venture. I recently had the pleasure of reconnecting with some friends of mine who started a new business called Quo. Quo started as a traditional apartment search site but quickly had to pivot to find a solid product/ market fit. After Quo experienced less than stellar demand from users at launch, the team took action, engaging focus groups and gaining feedback from prospective users. It took a fair amount of self-awareness and humility to absorb honest feedback, but for the Quo team, it paid off.

Throughout their research, a common theme seemed to occur repeatedly. Apartment renters struggled when it came to communicating with property managers, dealing with thousands of listings, and managing a complex process without an advocate or friend by their side. They took that feedback and realized that they were positioned to act as a personal apartment search concierge for their clients. The shift has been successful so far, and since introducing the new approach, Quo has expanded into new markets, including New York City.

Here's the moral of the story. If you're an entrepreneur who has put all your effort into creating a great product only to see mediocre demand from customers, don't lose hope. Instead, make sure that you take steps to expand your market, hook people early on, and focus attention on serving the right customer base. If you take a proactive approach to solving the issue and commit to adjusting strategies as you work toward your goals, you'll find yourself generating the demand your product deserves.

PART 2: SCALING YOUR BUSINESS

Starting a business is only the first hurdle entrepreneurs must overcome. The real challenges arrive when you're trying to scale your business. In this period of dramatic growth and maturity, entrepreneurs need to develop a new and more robust skill set. In this section, I'll explore the following:

- running your business;
- growing your business;
- funding your business;
- managing your people; and
- exiting your business.

RUNNING YOUR BUSINESS

A TYPICAL DAY IN THE LIFE OF A START-UP CEO

I've had the privilege of working closely with CEOs of all kinds throughout my career, from leaders of Fortune 500 companies to founders of private investment firms. The role of the start-up CEO, however, is different from anything I've ever seen. When you're leading a young company, you must live a life of balance. Strategy must be balanced with operations, and leadership must be balanced with a willingness to listen. It's truly a role unlike any other.

When I tell people that I'm the CEO of a fintech start-up, I'm often met with blank stares and questions of, "So what does that mean, exactly?" In today's environment, in which entrepreneurship is often idealized, there is still a bit of mystery surrounding exactly what a modern CEO does on a daily basis. Everyone is different, of course, and I can't speak for my peers, but I'm happy to give a glimpse in my routine.

TAKE THE TIME TO PLAN

My day usually starts right around six-thirty in the morning. By that time, I can be found at my local Starbucks drafting out a plan for the day. I like to have some time to myself, free of office distractions, in which to map out an agenda for what I want to accomplish each day. If I don't, I find that I fall victim to the whims of whatever random task pops up.

I typically draw up a grid divided into four sectors—team, strategy, product, and growth—and then list out the tasks that need to be accomplished in each area. This helps me make sure that I touch all the major aspects of my business and that I don't let anything slide.

TOUCH BASE WITH THE TEAM

I still have a relatively small team, so I'm able to engage with everyone one-on-one every day. Once I get into the office, I make the rounds and get a feel for where people stand.

The goal of these check-ins is twofold: first, it gives me the opportunity to see what everyone is working on and make sure that they're on track, and second, it enables me to see how people are feeling and address any issues they might have before they become real problems. I've found that challenges of all kinds are easier to deal with when you provide clear channels of communication.

COMMUNICATE WITH YOUR STAKEHOLDERS
After I check in with the team, there is usually a call with a member of my board or other stakeholder to talk strategy. I've found that this is the time for me to work on the big picture and deepen relationships with our investors. Even though I'm the CEO, I still have a boss. I work for my shareholders, and this is my time to engage with them.

ALWAYS FOCUS ON THE PRODUCT
Next, I spend time working on our product. This usually entails thinking about ways we can improve, soliciting feedback from clients, and working with my talented CTO. In a tech start-up, it is all too easy to designate everything as a priority. Of course, when everything is a top priority, nothing is. We brainstorm, debate, and ultimately make the tough decisions necessary for true prioritization.

DRIVING GROWTH
By this time, the day is starting to get away from me. We have institutional partners across the country, so I have to be mindful of time zones. I always start on the East Coast and work my way west. I have a motivated sales team that focuses on our core banking clients, but my COO and I tend to handle some of the larger strategic deals that don't fit into that category. Sometimes this means doing demos or crafting presentations. Other times I find myself going in for the sale, sharing our vision for the future, and trying to close deals.

THINKING AND WRITING
Running a company is not a nine-to-five job. The end of the typical workday marks the halfway point for me. After heading home for dinner and a bit of time with the family, I focus on writing and building the BodeTree

brand. I push myself to write every single day, and it is invaluable time. Much of this writing never sees the light of day, but some of it makes it all the way to the *Forbes* column I write. This is very much my time to reflect and decompress. It's when I think about what I've learned and what I can do better.

Running a company isn't always glamorous. In fact, it's often downright monotonous. But routine leads to efficiency and creates a sense of security inside of an organization. Sure, there are fire drills and crazy days, but in general, that's what a day in the life looks like for me.

How to Deal with Disappointment in Business

Entrepreneurship is a roller coaster ride unlike any other, especially for founders. When you think about a business, there are two kinds of capital: money and emotional investment. Founders usually have the highest emotional investment of anyone in the organization. After all, the business is their baby and—for entrepreneurs—life is work, and work is life. For better or worse, everything that happens to or in a business is somewhat personal.

When disappointment comes—and it always does—it's easy to let it get you down on a number of fronts. However, for the sake of the company, the team, and your sanity, you'll have to learn how to deal with the situation in a positive manner. I'm not an expert on many things, but one area where I have plenty of experience is dealing with disappointment. I'd like to share what I've learned over the years so that my fellow entrepreneurs are better equipped to deal with the challenges they face in their lives.

Stay Strong and Keep a Good Poker Face

Attitudes are highly contagious, especially inside small organizations. This is true on many fronts, but it's especially acute when you're dealing with the leader's attitude. If a team sees a leader in a depressive mood, it will spread like wildfire. It's critical for leaders to maintain a good poker face. I don't view this practice as a method of hiding the truth—far from it. Instead, it's a matter of not allowing your fleeting feelings to affect the morale of those around you. It sounds corny, but good leaders don't have the luxury of whining.

I've had plenty of experience dealing with disappointment over the course of my career. One incident in particular stands out in my mind. I had the opportunity to do a transformative deal with a group that I trusted, respected, and admired, and it ultimately fell through thanks to forces outside my control.

It was painful, but I realized that I could not allow my personal disappointment to affect my performance or the morale of my team members. The only way to deal with the disappointment was to recognize it, accept it, and move on to bigger and better things.

HANDLE THE SITUATION WITH GRACE

Receiving disappointing news is never fun, and it's all too easy to let emotions get the better of you. No matter how sad, frustrated, or angry you may feel in the moment, the ability to demonstrate grace under pressure is one of the most admirable qualities a leader can possess. However, it rarely comes naturally; it must be nurtured over time. When faced with disappointment, always seek to handle the situation with poise, understanding, and respect.

When I receive disappointing news, I strive to make sure that the other parties involved recognize my appreciation for all the work put in along the way. While things don't always go the way we want, when everyone involved handles the situation with honor, respect, and transparency, the future remains bright with opportunities to work together again. Handling the disappointment of the moment with grace and dignity goes a long way in cementing ongoing mutual respect.

KEEP MOVING FORWARD, NO MATTER WHAT

Business, like life and football, is a game of inches. As I've noted, most successful businesses are defined by the sum of all of the little decisions and interactions that happen each day, not by grand, strategic moves. This simple truth puts the responsibility on both leaders and teams to make every single moment count. When faced with disappointment, you can either crumple up in defeat or keep moving forward. Successful people demonstrate true grit and keep moving inch by inch, moment by moment, even in the face of disappointment and setbacks.

As for me? I'm committed to moving forward, no matter what comes my way. I have a strong team, a great product, and amazing backers. Would that deal that ultimately fell through have been fantastic for BodeTree and the other party? Absolutely. Did I let myself mourn the missed opportunity? No way. We redoubled our efforts and charged forward, stronger than ever.

How I Failed to Develop Our Culture, and How I Fixed It

There are many mistakes that you can (and likely will) make as an entrepreneur or leader, but the good news is that most can be fixed. Perhaps you've designed a product that doesn't fit the needs of the market, or you've guided your team toward the wrong distribution channel. These mistakes aren't the end of the world.

You can always pick yourself up, fix what went wrong, and keep moving forward with minimal long-term damage. However, there is one mistake that isn't easily fixed: neglecting your company's culture. The culture that you develop sets the tone for every interaction and decision in your company. If your company's culture isn't nurtured and starts to go sideways, the long-term effects can be devastating.

I'll be the first to admit that BodeTree has struggled when it comes to culture. It's not to say that our team members don't like what they do. After all, we're enjoying strong growth and making a difference for small-business owners across the country. However, I think my team members would be hard pressed to articulate the essence of our culture and describe its effect on what we do.

The inability to define our team's culture is itself a failure that can be traced directly back to me. Whether I'd like to admit it or not, the leader defines the culture and sets the tone for the entire organization. Over the past year, I've come to realize my failings and have committed to focusing on culture and cultivating it at every level of the organization. Fixing my mistakes in this area isn't easy, but I'm making progress. Here are the three major lessons I've learned so far.

You're Never Too Small to Worry about Culture

For the first year and a half of our existence, the team consisted primarily of my cofounder and me. Matt and I had a lot in common and had worked together for several years before starting the company, so the topic of our corporate culture rarely came up.

After all, we got along just fine and were so busy building our product that abstract things like culture seemed unimportant. We never defined our company's ethos and pushed off conversations about our identity until we had a larger team. However, even as our team started to grow, culture continued to take a back seat to more pressing matters.

In retrospect, I should have started with a strong focus on the culture that we wanted to foster at the company from day one. Hoping that our culture would grow organically was a mistake. For us, it simply never manifested itself the way we wanted. There was no magic moment where everything came together and we collectively realized why we all wanted to dedicate ourselves to building this company. I've since realized that culture has to be defined, guided, and nurtured from the very beginning if it is to take root.

REMEMBER THAT THE LITTLE THINGS MATTER

How your team members handle the little challenges and decisions they face day in and day out defines and reinforces a company's culture. Put another way, small and seemingly innocuous things can have an oversize effect on an organization. For example, we pride ourselves on being a transparent organization when it comes to major decisions. Whether we're making changes to our product, shifting our distribution strategy, or looking to expand the team, we make sure that everyone knows what's going on and why.

However, there have been incidents when our innocent actions have been perceived as being secretive or opaque. Sometimes it's closed-door meetings or hushed phone calls. Other times, it's the use of private chat rather than group channels in our Slack account. While each instance can be easily explained and is more often than not perfectly justified, the overall perception of such actions hurts the organization.

Old habits are hard to break, and I'm the worst offender when it comes to neglecting the small things. I still am far more inclined to send a private message to a member of the team rather than post it in a group chat. I'm also the type to instinctively close my door whenever I get a phone call. Still, I'm trying to change my behavior and lead by example. I realize that perception and the negative effect of these actions can build up over time and lead to a culture of distrust.

Culture Is Defined by the Weakest Link

I recently came across a powerful image that management consultant Kathy van de Laar shared on LinkedIn. The idea put forth was that the culture of any organization is shaped by the worst behavior the leader is willing to tolerate. The statement resonated with me and helped me realize that our struggles with defining a culture were my fault and no one else's. After all, I've tolerated cultural missteps from day one.

I now realize that it's the leader's job to serve as the tireless defender of company culture, holding everyone (especially yourself) accountable when there are shortcomings. In fact, the focus needs to be so strong that the chief executive officer should almost be called the chief culture officer instead. It's tough to create and maintain a strong company culture from day one. It's even harder to play catch-up after neglecting it.

Still, no matter what mistakes have been made in the past, good leaders recognize their mistakes, make adjustments, and keep moving forward. Culture isn't easily developed or fixed, but that doesn't mean that leaders can continue to ignore it.

HOW TO STAY PATIENT AND PRODUCTIVE, EVEN WHEN WAITING

It's been said that patience is a virtue, and like most virtues, it doesn't come easily. When you're a small, fast-growing company that frequently partners with large, slow-moving organizations, you often find yourself in a "hurry up and wait" scenario.

The fundamental mismatch in the natural velocity of start-ups versus established companies can be frustrating. Unless you invest in developing the virtue of patience and learn to take advantage of excess time, the never-ending waiting will drive you mad.

I've struggled with this firsthand. We work with financial institutions and other gigantic public companies all the time. Our sales cycle for these institutional accounts ranges anywhere from eight to twelve months, and it isn't uncommon to have months pass between milestones. At first, this elongated timeline made it difficult to focus and maintain productivity.

After all, each client has unique needs, and there can be a strong temptation to delay decisions until you have certainty. This often leads to a situation where you have long periods of inaction followed by brief flurries of activity, which can be difficult on teams. Fortunately, my team members and I have learned how to manage this challenge and turn it into an advantage.

LESSON ONE: BE BOLD, AND DEFINE THE EXPERIENCE FOR YOUR CUSTOMERS

When you're forced to wait for customers and partners, it's easy to become paralyzed when making decisions. After all, you don't know precisely how they will react to a situation, so the temptation to simply postpone important decisions can be strong. Unfortunately, this decision paralysis is often incredibly damaging for two reasons.

First, it causes your team members to second-guess all their decisions, making it almost impossible for them to stay productive. Second, it leads to fragmented and weak execution. Early on at BodeTree, we waited until we had absolute clarity from partners and clients before crafting a go-to-market plan. While this was well intended, it meant that we had to rush to reinvent the wheel at the last minute—every time. By waiting for perfect clarity before moving forward, we ended up going wide instead of deep, and it simply didn't work.

Ultimately, we realized that if we were going to be successful, we were going to have to make decisions without perfect clarity and define the experience for ourselves. This shift from reactive to proactive decision making enabled us to create a deep, high-quality work product that we believed in. By taking a strong stance, making bold decisions, and bringing a completed package to our clients, we were able to define the experience from start to finish. This enabled us to remain focused, productive, and well ahead of the curve regardless of how slowly our partners moved.

LESSON TWO: USE EXTRA TIME TO FOCUS ON THE DETAILS

When it comes to execution, the devil is in the details. Seemingly innocuous things like product messaging and e-mail design can have a disproportionate effect on the ultimate success of your product. When you're rushed to execute, it's often easy to overlook these details. Fortunately, the time you gain while waiting for others to get back to you allows you to focus on things that might otherwise get lost in the shuffle.

One of the early marketing mistakes that I made at BodeTree was to oversimplify our approach to customer engagement. I wrongly assumed that I knew what people cared about and which messages resonated with a broad audience. I wasted so much time waiting to hear back from clients that when things finally accelerated, I went with a "good enough" approach to customer marketing and engagement. It was only after I learned to take advantage of the waiting time that I was able to focus on these details and improve. Downtime is a gift; it enables you to focus on all of the little details that make your product truly exceptional.

LESSON THREE: STAY POSITIVE AND KEEP MOVING FORWARD—NO MATTER WHAT

Long sales cycles can be emotionally hard on teams. The long gaps in between milestones often lead to insecurity and anxiety. That's why it is incredibly important to make sure that you use these gaps to your advantage by constantly moving the process forward. Psychological momentum has a huge effect on the success of a business.

If your team feels productive, motivated, and positive, this reflects in your interactions with customers and partners alike. At times, the temptation to give in to boredom will be strong, but it's imperative that leaders keep this from happening.

The ability to wait isn't particularly valuable. However, the wisdom to transform thoughtful patience into productivity and momentum is what separates winners from losers. Take advantage of downtime to define the customer experience, focus on details, and foster positivity in your team. If you do, you'll find that you can transform long sales cycles and waiting into a major competitive advantage.

How to Turn Obstacles into Opportunities

Entrepreneurs often find that the only constants in life are problems. Obstacles are to be dreaded, leading only to stress, anxiety, and self-doubt—at least, that's what we've been conditioned to think.

But history is littered with examples of people who have managed to overcome and thrive on the struggles they experience. Why is it that a select few seem to succeed where the rest of us fail repeatedly? The answer lies in a thought expressed by a Roman emperor, Marcus Aurelius, eighteen hundred years ago, who said, "The impediment to action advances action. What stands in the way becomes the way."

Simply put, the struggles we face offer us a path to growth and success. It's a counterintuitive concept, to be sure, but it is perhaps the single most important concept that any entrepreneur can learn: how to embrace challenges.

Bad Luck Is the Opportunity You're Looking For

I was introduced to this mind-set by a successful relative. In his first leadership role, he found himself routinely frustrated and discouraged by the problems that seemed to constantly pop up. Expensive equipment frequently failed, employees caused problems, and clients were always upset about one thing or another. He was convinced that he could be successful—if only he could catch a break from all the bad luck coming his way.

After one particularly challenging period, however, he had an epiphany. He realized that while he couldn't control his luck, he could control how he reacted. Perhaps his bad luck wasn't bad luck at all but actually an opportunity to prove himself. His entire mentality changed that day. Instead of dreading problems, he began to actively seek them out. "Where's the next problem?" became his personal mantra, and it became the basis for his entire business philosophy.

Today, I try to practice that same spirit both at work and in my personal life. It's a belief that colors everything I do.

PRACTICE, PRACTICE, AND PRACTICE SOME MORE

The temptation to despair or blame others for things is often strong, but it can be overcome—with practice.

In any given business situation, the only thing that you truly have control over is yourself. As difficult as it may seem, you always have the choice to recognize the obstacle for what it is, find something positive, and work like hell to push through it.

My own personal journey to this realization was not an easy one. As far back as I can remember, I've been prone to anxiety and worry. The prospect of the unknown or uncontrollable petrified me and prevented me from taking action. I always admired people who could keep their cool in the worst of situations, turning challenges into opportunities and emerging stronger than before. I thought that this was something innate: you were either born with it or not. The truth, of course, is that this grit is a learned behavior that can be refined over time.

My lesson in developing grit started shortly after I graduated college when I took a job at a business valuation consultancy that had a unique corporate culture. By unique, of course, I mean toxic and horrifying. It was, without a doubt, the most trying time in my life. Every time I made an error or was belittled by partners, a part of me wanted to run. The temptation to quit was strong, but I forced myself to endure. I would leave the company, but only on my terms. I resolved to handle every insult, threat, and stressor that could be thrown at me with grit and determination.

No one would control how I felt or responded. It wasn't easy, and I often fell short of my own expectations, but I didn't give up. I practiced self-control and managed to stick it out long enough to gain skills that would serve me well in the future.

YOU ARE THE SECRET TO YOUR OWN SUCCESS

The way to nurture grit and capitalize on the opportunities that challenges offer is to cultivate an unshakable will to thrive. That's really all there is to it. It's both the easiest and the most difficult thing in the world. You simply have to want it badly enough to constantly push forward. Will you fail at times? Absolutely. Will it be easy? Never. The only thing you can do is keep at it.

IDEAS TAKE HOLD; DICTATES DO NOT

Of all the common misconceptions about leadership, one of the most pernicious is the idea that it takes a strong and aggressive personality to guide a team. No matter how far we progress as a society, and despite all the advances in modern management technique, people still seem to expect a certain degree of old-fashioned military-style leadership inside organizations.

Grand announcements and dictates rarely prove to be effective in the modern workplace. Instead, successful leadership is all about subtlety. In fact, when leaders do things right, the people they lead won't be sure that they themselves have done anything at all.

Ideas are a lot like viruses. They take hold, spread quickly, and evolve to suit their environment. The human mind is conditioned to value organic ideas and reject dictates. Smart leaders recognize this and can get ideas to take hold organically. When people see the natural generation and spread of an idea, they're much more likely to act on it than if the idea had been forced on them.

Helping ideas to take hold and spread organically is about listening and understanding, not about manipulation. Good leaders listen to what their team members say and find ways to help them reach the desired conclusion on their own. The truth is that people are often more aligned than they appear to be.

It's only when we anchor on ideas and try to force thoughts on others that people resist. It takes a certain sense of humility for leaders to succeed with this approach. If they do it right, all credit and praise goes to the people they lead. While this can be difficult for some, I've found that the best leaders are the people who can take pride in the success of the team they nurture.

POOR COMMUNICATION IS AT THE ROOT OF ALL CONFLICT

I'm a firm believer that poor communication is to blame for most organizational conflicts. Communication is tricky—it takes tact, compassion, and concerted effort to be effective. At BodeTree, we haven't always done a good job of fostering truly effective internal communication.

In the past, we've allowed misunderstandings and incorrect perceptions to fester far longer than they should. Left unchecked, this lack of communication leads to personal conflict and poor decision making across an organization.

I've learned that it's the job of the leader to pay close attention to the way a team communicates, shining a light on areas of discord early. The CEO's role is that of facilitator, confidant, and counselor for the team. It takes a fair amount of self-awareness and empathy to develop the necessary skill set, but once honed, it is invaluable for an organization. If a leader can step in and facilitate healthy communication at the right time, teams have a much better chance of resolving issues quickly and subtly before they get out of control.

SUBTLE PRESSURE CAN MOVE MOUNTAINS

If you want to move a mountain, you don't need heavy machinery and explosives. All you need is the constant, unyielding pressure of a stream. With enough consistency and time, even the subtlest of pressures can create incredible results. The same principle can be applied in businesses. There have been instances at BodeTree when I have fundamentally disagreed with the direction that my team wanted to take. However, I've found that when I make a quick, unequivocal pronouncement about what I believe to be right, people struggle to accept it. Instead, the subtle and consistent reinforcement of an idea has the most significant effect.

Leadership is not easy. It takes consistency, humility, and empathy to successfully guide a modern workforce. The old model of top-down, dictatorial management is no longer effective. Instead, leaders must learn to foster ideas within their team, know when to facilitate communication, and exhibit a subtle yet consistent pressure to guide their team forward.

Embracing the Uncomfortable Parts of Start-Up Life

There are many aspects of entrepreneurship that are, frankly, uncomfortable. From having difficult conversations with employees to raising capital, doing what is right for the company can force a leader outside his or her comfort zone.

Entrepreneurs and leaders often struggle in these situations because they want to be too polite, indirect, or nonconfrontational. However, successful leaders must learn to embrace the uncomfortable to do what is right for their company.

Just Do It

Of all the things that a leader has to contend with in start-up life, I've found that the process of raising capital was always one of the most uncomfortable. Once, during a conversation with a friend and mentor, I remarked that I hated asking people for money.

My mentor's response was one that I'll never forget: *get over it*. In short, I was told to suck it up and do what was right for the company. I had to embrace the uncomfortable nature of the conversation and just move forward.

As an entrepreneur, you're not just representing yourself in conversations. You're representing your entire organization. You no longer have the luxury of hiding behind your insecurities. It sounds simplistic, but the only choice you have when it comes to making the tough decisions is just to do it.

Remember the Value That You Bring

During our conversation, my mentor zeroed in on one particular phrase I used. He admonished me for saying that I was "asking people for money." That, he pointed out, was a damaging and false mind-set. He advised me to stop thinking of it as asking people for money and instead focus on sharing a lucrative opportunity with people.

This didn't mean that I needed to become a carnival barker, going overboard on the self-promotion. Instead, he pointed out that we have a great product, solid team, and tremendous upside for potential investors. Sharing the opportunity to participate in the upside was, once again, simply business. By shying away from something I perceived to be uncomfortable, I was undervaluing the very thing my team had worked so hard to build.

It's important to remember the value that you bring to the table in any scenario. When I first started contributing to *Forbes* and MSNBC, my nagging insecurities made me feel like I wasn't qualified to have such a platform. Over time, however, I realized that my experiences building a company from scratch offered valuable insights that benefit a broader audience. That realization gave me the confidence to push through my discomfort and accomplish my goals.

It Gets Easier

The funny thing about embracing uncomfortable situations is that the more you do it, the easier it gets. The first time you push yourself outside of your comfort zone can be nerve-racking at first, but when you're done, it usually proves to be less painful than you expected. As you continue pushing forward, you'll find that the anxiety and discomfort simply melt away.

My advice is to start small and build up your immunity to uncomfortable situations. Find a few opportunities for which the stakes aren't particularly high, like a public speaking engagement in front of a small crowd or an investment pitch session with a trusted adviser.

Things might not go your way, but regardless of the outcome, you'll start breaking down your fears. As you build up to more and more important situations, you'll find that getting outside your comfort zone isn't as terrifying as it once seemed.

Uncomfortable situations are simply part of the entrepreneurial journey, but you can learn to embrace the challenge and, in doing so, overcome your fears. The trick is simply to commit to action, remember the value you bring, and keep moving forward no matter what.

GROWING YOUR BUSINESS

SOMETIMES YOU HAVE TO BURN THE BOATS

In 1519, eleven ships carrying six hundred Spaniards landed on an inland plateau that would one day be known as Mexico. Their goal was to conquer an empire that had amassed a massive fortune of gold, silver, and precious gems. However, when attempted with just six hundred men, most of whom were vastly undersupplied, conquering the vast Aztec empire seemed like an impossible task.

However, Cortés was undeterred. Rather than charge forward as soon as they landed in Mexico, Cortés gathered his men on the beach and promptly ordered the burning of the ships in which they had just arrived, effectively destroying their only escape route. The only choice left was to push forward—and succeed.

ELIMINATE YOUR SAFETY NET

Taking the underlying morality of Cortés's actions out of the equation for a moment, it's easy to see how many entrepreneurs often find themselves in similar circumstances. To be a start-up is to contend with a constant sense of being outmanned, outgunned, and outplanned. On the surface, the idea of a small, often poorly supplied team making waves in the world may seem just as ludicrous as trying to conquer an empire with only six hundred men, but they're really not that different.

Sometimes burning your ships and eliminating your safety net is the only way to inspire team members to push forward in the face of daunting odds. My team and I did it at BodeTree, and it was the best decision we ever made.

BE PREPARED TO PIVOT

When we first launched BodeTree, our plan was to sell our products directly to small-business owners, helping them cut out the proverbial middleman when it came to managing their finances. We charged down this path for several years and achieved moderate success. However, we knew that in order to gain the scale we were looking for, we would have to explore other options.

We ultimately chose to shift our focus away from direct-to-consumer sales and toward working with large institutional partners. This move enabled us to gain scale rapidly and grow the business into what it is today. The shift was not going to be an easy one, and we knew that the sales cycle for selling to institutions could be long and painful.

At first, we merely dipped our toe into the market. Our institutional sales channel was, to be frank, an afterthought at first. We continued to support and market our direct presence and thought that we could serve two masters. For us, the direct channel was a safety net. If selling to institutional partners proved to be too difficult or time-consuming, we could always fall back on what we had built. We had our ships anchored in the bay, providing an escape route if the going got tough. As a result, we failed to commit fully to our new channel.

Once I realized this, I knew what had to be done. We would have to burn our ships if we were to have any chance of succeeding. It was a terrifying decision to make, because we had invested so much into that initial effort. We had designed all our marketing materials, brand presence, and technical features around the idea of selling directly to the small-business owner. To back away from this decision meant reworking our entire approach and making changes to the team we had assembled.

IT WON'T BE EASY

The decision was made in early 2014 and proved to be just as difficult as we had feared. We had to replace team members and refocus the entire organization. We continued to allow direct sign-ups and to support our existing customers, but we effectively shut down all our marketing efforts centered around that channel.

Our mantra became "all institutions, all the time." To make matters worse, sales did not start rolling in. In fact, they stalled for months on end. The team grew nervous, and investors questioned the all-in approach we were taking. In spite of this, we maintained our course and never looked back. Over time, things started to turn around. Then they started to accelerate faster than any of us could have expected.

It was our decision to "burn our ships" and commit fully to our institutional strategy that enabled us to persevere and eventually thrive. Had we had the safety net of our direct efforts waiting in the wings, we never would have been able to succeed. A primal response surfaces only when a person is faced with a life-or-death situation. Too often, we limit ourselves by holding on to our escape routes and safety nets. Sometimes you just have to burn the ships in order to move forward.

WHEN SELLING, AUTHENTICITY MATTERS MOST

The nature of sales has always fascinated me. When BodeTree started to take off and launch into a period of rapid expansion, I had to make decisions about just what kind of sales organization we wanted to be.

The culture of a sales team, much like the culture of the organization as a whole, is determined by the expectations, decisions, and incentives put in place by members of leadership. A company's sales team is the tip of the spear, representing the very real and very public face of the organization. Its conduct not only affects its ability to drive growth, but it also colors the perception of the organization in the market.

If there were one word I'd like to see used to describe our sales culture, it would be *authentic*. The very nature of sales is evolving, and it will be the champions of authenticity who will come out ahead.

BE A PROBLEM SOLVER, NOT A PUSHER

For many people, the topic of sales conjures up images of pushy car salesmen or the boiler rooms made famous in *Glengarry Glen Ross*. There is a prevailing yet often unspoken notion in the market that salespeople are ruthless sharks, motivated only by the prospect of commissions. As a result, many would-be customers approach sales conversations defensively and with a great deal of suspicion.

These "hard sell" tactics are as antiquated as they are ineffective. Going forward, successful sales professionals will be problem solvers, not pushers. We're witnessing the nature of sales transforming into a solution-centric process that more closely mirrors the world of consulting. Our sales team always puts the customer's needs first, adding exceptional value and becoming trusted advisers to our clients. In doing so, we seek to distance ourselves from the negative stereotypes of sales and carve out a unique niche in the market.

ADD VALUE, EVEN IF IT MEANS LOSING THE SALE

This is more than a mere aspiration; it's a fundamental part of our culture. Once I tagged along with one of my sales executives to a meeting with a decent-size bank out in California. The bank executives were sharp and responsive, but it was clear that the bulk of their interest centered around an ancillary feature of our system rather than the core. As I listened to them describe their needs, I realized that we wouldn't be the best fit for them.

As I conferred with my team, we found ourselves faced with a tricky situation. The sales process was moving along nicely, and we all agreed that we could very well push forward with our solution and sign the deal. That would be great for our bottom line, but we all knew there were other solutions out there that would be a better fit for the client's needs.

I'm exceedingly proud of how my team responded to the situation. Rather than push forward, we opted instead to refer our client to one of our competitors. We made it clear that our competitor simply would be a more appropriate solution for the bank's needs at this time. We put the bank's needs first—no strings attached.

The client responded with disbelief at first. The bank's managers had never encountered a sales team that recommended a competitor's solution instead of its own. However, once they got over their initial shock, they were incredibly grateful. They immediately saw our team as a group of authentic and dedicated problem solvers, and they have sung our praises throughout the industry.

REMEMBER THAT WHAT GOES AROUND COMES AROUND

Even though we lost the deal, we earned the client's trust and respect. Since that time, its managers have continued to reach out to us proactively, asking our advice and input on a number of their decisions. To them, our team comprises advisers and industry experts rather than sales executives. I'm convinced that that will pay dividends in the future, both with this client and among others with which it interacts.

Our approach is as simple as it is counterintuitive. Call it karma if you must, but we believe that in business, what goes around comes around. In a world that has been jaded by pushy and self-centered sales processes, an authentic, consultative approach is a breath of fresh air. It may result in losing a few battles here or there, but those organizations that put their clients first—no matter what—are all but guaranteed to win the war.

BEWARE OF BUSINESS SABOTEURS

Business-to-business sales are tricky, due in no small part to the number of people who tend to be involved in the process. In any B2B situation, you have the key stakeholders, their direct reports, and then a legion of operational people who help with due diligence and implementation.

Occasionally, strange things happen when a significant number of people get involved in these situations, especially when they come from big companies. For some reason, there are often individuals who want to stand athwart progress yelling, "Stop!" Sometimes their objection arises from a valid concern about the issue at hand. More often, however, their opposition comes because they feel threatened—or because it wasn't their idea.

Ideally, these situations are rectified with clear and honest communication, and the process can roll forward. Unfortunately, we don't live in an ideal world, and more often than not, people will resort to trying to disrupt the process stealthily.

I've had to deal with business saboteurs more often than I'd like to admit. Fortunately, I've learned a thing or two about handling them over the years.

FIRST AND FOREMOST, TAKE A LOOK AT YOURSELF AND ACCEPT RESPONSIBILITY

When BodeTree first started out, we had a small sales channel that focused on accounting firms and small-business advisers. The firms we dealt with loved the platform's potential and the efficiency gains it could provide. The firm's front-line employees, however, felt extremely threatened by the system because we were automating large parts of their jobs.

When the first firm we were working with decided to test the system ahead of signing the contract, it looked to these front-line employees for help. Understandably, these people were absolutely merciless when it came to even the smallest of bugs or customer service issues. They absolutely savaged us in an attempt to scuttle the deal.

As a young and inexperienced founder at the time, I was absolutely livid. While there were glitches and technical issues that were encountered, the individuals who were complaining flat-out lied about my team's responsiveness and the level of support that was provided. My first reaction was to let loose a barrage of angry e-mails and comments, refuting each point with blistering precision. Fortunately, I managed to cool down and respond far more intelligently.

Rather than question the integrity of the individuals, I chose to accept responsibility for the very real glitches that they encountered. We identified the issues, resolved the problems, and put in place new safeguards to prevent them from happening again. It wasn't easy to force down the raging fury that burned just beneath the surface, but the decision showed that we were an organization that behaved with grace and maturity.

RECOGNIZE THAT PERCEPTION IS REALITY

Now, we weren't out of the woods yet. While I did my best to manage the situation with the firm's leadership and make progress, much of the damage had already been done. I quickly learned that perception is, in fact, reality for many people. There is a certain inertia inside of large organizations to begin with, and many times stakeholders are simply waiting for a bump in the road in order to stop the entire process.

This was a harsh realization for me on a personal level. Even though the situation seemed blatantly unfair, the deal was all but dead. Faced with this unfortunate reality, I had to figure out how to respond.

RESPOND WITH FACTS, AND DON'T GET ANGRY

There was a strong temptation to go out in a blaze of glory, employing a scorched-earth policy that would have felt good in the moment but that would have left a lasting legacy in the marketplace. Instead, I simply presented the facts as they stood, demonstrating my team's responsiveness and politely refuting some of the false assertions some of the company's employees had leveled.

I resisted the urge to get angry, as tempting as it was to do so. The deal ended not with a bang but with a whimper. It simply melted away over time. It was a personal loss for me and a loss for the firm. However, it was a valuable learning experience that has helped shape me as a leader.

Business saboteurs are very real, and they are very dangerous. Unfortunately, there are individuals in large organizations (in all organizations, for that matter) who embrace the status quo and who want to avoid change at all costs. However, giving into your base desires and lashing out is never the right move. Instead, leaders must accept responsibility, recognize that perception is often reality, and respond with facts, not anger.

Sometimes you will lose a deal, and sometimes it will come down to fundamentally unfair reasons. That reality is out of your control. However, your behavior and reputation are fully in your control. Deals come and go, but dignity and maturity stay with you forever.

RISK NEVER GOES AWAY; IT EVOLVES

One thing I've learned along my entrepreneurial journey is that business is evolutionary. Risk, in particular, never really goes away; it just evolves and takes new and different forms. To understand the evolutionary nature of risk is to understand the life cycle of your business. Good leaders understand how risk changes and can focus their skills and efforts accordingly.

While there are an infinite number of different risk phases that a business will go through over the course of its life, there are three main "epochs" to which every business owner can relate. Each has its set of challenges and opportunities, and it's incredibly important for entrepreneurs to recognize where they stand among them.

EXISTENTIAL RISK

The first risk epoch is existential in nature. This occurs during the early stages of business, when entrepreneurs have to prove out the viability of their product or service. During this period, the primary focus of the business is the determination of whether your product is desired, valued, and functional.

The period of existential risk is when most businesses fail. It takes a lot of hard work, perseverance, and luck to survive. Businesses at this stage are prerevenue and incur many start-up costs. Investors who choose to participate at this stage shoulder a good deal of risk and, as a result, generally take a much larger portion of the equity. Entrepreneurs in this phase of the business have to remain mindful of the unproven nature of their creation and act with an appropriate level of humility and caution.

EXECUTION RISK

If there is one mistake that I've seen many entrepreneurs make time and time again, it's harboring the false assumption that existential risk is the only risk that matters. While the need to prove out a concept's viability is obvious, it is by no means the be-all and end-all.

The second epoch is characterized by execution risk, in which businesses work to scale what they've created. This is where the entrepreneurs are separated from the operators. Some people revel in creating something from nothing and have less interest in actually running a business. Those types of entrepreneurs tend to struggle during the execution phase of the business.

SUSTAINABILITY RISK

The third, and arguably the most difficult, risk epoch is all about maintaining the viability of the business you've created. This is the point when the sins of the past come to the surface and when seemingly solid companies can collapse with little warning.

Before founding BodeTree, I worked at the Apollo Education Group. Apollo owns and operates institutions in the for-profit education space, and it recently experienced a dramatic collapse. After years of hypergrowth, fantastic margins, and industry-defining advances, the University of Phoenix (Apollo's flagship institution) is being sold to a group of investors for a mere $1.1 billion dollars. The reasons for Apollo's fall are all too common: hubris and greed.

In an attempt to keep growth rolling at the pace to which investors had become accustomed, the organization pursued strategies and avenues that were ill-advised at best and unethical at worst. In short, members of management failed to ensure that the business had a stable and sustainable future, leading to the organization's eventual collapse.

Like most things in life, business risk is both nuanced and evolutionary. Entrepreneurs and business leaders need to recognize this and understand in what phase they find themselves. The best leaders are the ones who can successfully evolve alongside their company and guide it to success.

There Are No Shortcuts to Sustainable Growth

For years now, the entire start-up world has marveled at the rise of the so-called unicorns, companies that seem to grow at breakneck speeds and achieve unprecedented valuations. Among entrepreneurs, companies such as Uber, Zenefits, and Theranos have represented a form of "start-up nirvana" that everyone has striven to recreate.

Recently, however, we've begun to see cracks in the façades of these unicorns. Theranos, the former darling of the biotech world, has been faced with crisis after crisis, and in early 2016 another scandal rocked Zenefits, once hailed as the fastest-growing software company of all time.

This has been an interesting phenomenon to watch unfold. As the founder of a software company that focuses on serving small business, I've often been frustrated by—and, frankly, jealous of—the quick growth that many technology companies enjoy. At BodeTree, every single customer we have has been won the hard way, and I've been guilty of thinking that our slow yet steady approach lacks some of the elusive "unicorn magic." However, I've come to realize the simple truth: when it comes to creating sustainable, long-term growth, there are simply no shortcuts.

Winning with Early Adopters Is Easy

So-called early adopters are appropriately named, to say the least. These are individuals and companies that represent the most forward-thinking and creative customers your company will ever encounter. In the world of technology, there is a very strong community of early adopters, nearly all of whom tend to be young, educated, and relatively affluent. Early adopters are wowed by slick design and tend to be very forgiving when it comes to user experience.

Many companies have perfected the art of focusing on early adopters and as a result tend to see explosive growth in the early years of operation. Unfortunately, this growth can give founders a false view of reality, leading them to believe that winning over the middle-stage and late adopters will be just as easy. In reality, this couldn't be further from the truth.

WINNING OVER THE MIDDLE-STAGE AND LATE ADOPTERS IS A DIFFERENT STORY

I tend to believe that companies run into problems when they start to pursue customers who aren't early adopters. For teams, reaching this stage of the business is like running into a brick wall. It's as painful as it is jarring. These customers are less forgiving and are often difficult to reach. The "cool factor" of a product doesn't faze them in the least, and they're quick to question everything from its purpose to your messaging.

At BodeTree, we work with banks and other financial institutions to connect with small businesses. This institutional approach has provided us with the ability to gain access to a large number of small businesses, but it's always a challenge to find ways to convert these organizations into fully engaged and active users.

My team and I have learned that you have to get creative to connect with these types of users at scale. A cool brand and slick interface aren't enough. You have to fight for every user and get comfortable with more traditional "analog" methods of marketing. Even though we're a web application, we rely on multichannel methods of winning over customers, including brochures, direct mail, and even in-branch collateral, to win over customers.

This is a totally different approach than what works for tech-savvy early adopters, and it can be difficult to deal with. When confronted with these challenges, fast-growing companies get desperate, and that's when they start to make bad decisions. They cut corners, betray their values, and adopt a grow-at-all costs mentality that almost always comes back to bite them.

THE PATH TO VICTORY IS LONG AND PAINFUL

I often think back to a story about legendary movie producer Jerry Weintraub. Weintraub was fond of telling the story of how he kept a flock of plastic pink flamingoes in the grass near the entrance of his Hollywood office. When asked about the unique design choice, he responded that he kept them there to remind everyone that it's the mainstream public, not the Hollywood elite, who determine whether a movie is a hit. The same holds true for tech companies.

Sustainable growth doesn't come from early adopters and cool technology. It comes from the ability to slog it out with the middle-stage and late adopters, and that takes work. There are no shortcuts when it comes to serving these individuals. It takes patience, creativity, and, most important, persistence to crack that nut. The worst thing a company can do is try to cut corners in the pursuit of rapid growth. When that happens, you break the trust that exists between brand and customer, and that trust is not easily repaired.

I expect we will see more so-called unicorns stumble as they are forced to move beyond their base of early adopters. When that happens, they'll start to realize that when it comes to creating sustainable growth, there are no shortcuts.

THE ART OF NEGOTIATING WITH NUANCE

Much has been written about the art of negotiation, but few people recognize that negotiation isn't always a zero-sum game. Sometimes you find yourself having to negotiate with team members or strategic partners who will play a vital long-term role in your organization.

These situations require a unique and more nuanced approach to ensure that the relationship remains strong long after the negotiations have concluded. In my role as CEO, I often deal with these types of negotiations, and I have learned some valuable lessons about the nuances of negotiation and maintaining the integrity of relationships, even under difficult circumstances.

KEEP YOUR GREED IN CHECK

Greed is a trait that everyone demonstrates but that very few recognize in themselves. Unfortunately, nothing can destroy a relationship more quickly than a greed-driven negotiation. If one party pushes for too much or is too aggressive, a relationship can be irreparably damaged.

When it comes to the second type of negotiating—in which both parties hope to maintain a working relationship well beyond the bargaining table—it's important to remember that these situations are about future success, not short-term wins. It takes a special skill to recognize greedy behavior and stop it before it gets out of control.

This style of negotiation can be difficult to master, because no matter how hard you try, emotions inevitably influence your actions. The temptation to squeeze a partner for a better deal or to emerge "victorious" in a negotiation can be strong, and self-awareness and humility are required to resist it.

DON'T OVERPLAY YOUR HAND

Perhaps the best advice for engaging in a strategic negotiation is not to gamble with anything that you can't afford to lose. When you play hardball with another party, you have to recognize that your counterpart can simply walk away.

Ultimately, successful partner negotiations require three things. First, both parties need to recognize the nature of the negotiation itself. If you have to work with each other going forward, it's important to recognize that the negotiation cannot be a zero-sum game. Both sides need to walk away feeling aligned and motivated to move forward. Second, it's important to maintain perspective throughout the process. If one party gets greedy or behaves poorly throughout the negotiation, the working relationship may be irreparably damaged.

Finally, never gamble with something that you cannot afford to lose. Inherent in any negotiation is the risk of one party's simply walking away. All too often people get comfortable in a relationship and overplay their hand in negotiations. When this happens, they run the risk of losing everything, and that is the worst outcome of all.

HOW TO BUILD BUSINESS PARTNERSHIPS THAT LAST

For start-ups and small businesses, the opportunity to partner with large companies can seem like an easy path to success. Your scrappy little enterprise brings the innovative solution, and the sleepy, established behemoth brings capital and distribution. What could possibly go wrong? Unfortunately, it's never quite that simple when it comes to building successful and lasting partnerships.

BodeTree provides a simple yet powerful financial management platform for small businesses, filling a need felt by over 90 percent of those businesses across the United States. As a result, we've had the opportunity to partner with much larger and more established organizations, from major consumer software companies to large financial institutions, who are looking to better engage with the small-business market. Some of these partnerships have been wildly successful, and others have failed to get off the ground. Regardless of how it turned out, each one taught me important lessons about approaching and managing partnerships.

PRESENT A COMPELLING VISION FOR THE FUTURE

For start-ups and small businesses, it can be difficult to convince a large company to enter into a mutually beneficial partnership. After all, it's usually the smaller company that generally has more to gain in the relationship. It's not enough to have a complementary product or to serve a similar market; you have to present a compelling long-term vision for how the partnership will serve both sides' strategic goals.

The team and I once showed a financial institution with which we wanted to partner how we could revolutionize its digital banking strategy and helped it understand what that could mean for the organization and the industry as a whole. It wasn't the features and functionality of our product that convinced the client to partner—it was the shared strategic vision we presented.

Our approach was heavy on the visuals and boiled down the message into two simple diagrams that illustrated the client's current market position and where it could be postpartnership. We were careful to present the images digitally at first, introducing the concepts as we spoke so that the partners in attendance were forced to focus, rather than skipping ahead in a printed document. Only after the meeting was over did we circulate a simplified print version of the diagrams to the attendees.

Remember That Time Is of the Essence

Large organizations have two speeds: slow and slower. If you sit back and let the other side drive the process, chances are that nothing will get done. Even worse, constantly pestering your contacts on the other side to move forward is annoying at best and potentially damaging at worst. So how do you get your partners to take action? I've learned that the only way to get things moving is to create a genuine sense of urgency.

To do this, you have to understand your partner's organization and culture and find ways to focus on what matters to them. For BodeTree, we learned this when we realized that many of our partners were facing regulatory pressure to better serve small business. We were able to frame our conversations in the context of this pressure and use that to drive action.

Be Realistic, but Don't Undervalue Your Contribution

Finally, it's all too easy to undervalue your company's own contribution to the partnership. It can be tempting to give too much away when negotiating the economics or workload of the deal. Remember, if you're having partnership discussions, it's happening because the other side sees value in what you do. Outlining reasonable expectations and maintaining the value of your contribution not only ensures that the partnership is equitable but also signals to the other side that the relationship is something that it should be excited about.

This doesn't mean that you have to have a signed agreement right off the bat. Instead, it's a function of how you present yourself, your company, and your product. Projecting an aura of confidence and value goes a long way in helping guide the relationship down the right path.

It has been incredibly important for BodeTree, as an emerging company, to seek out partnerships that can be leveraged to dramatically accelerate our growth. These "moonshot" moments have helped us refine our product, marketing, and customer experience in short order. By sharing a defined vision for how to serve small business, we've been able to partner with some of the largest organizations in the market today.

However, we've learned firsthand just how important it is to ensure that the partnership is structured in such a way that it's mutually beneficial and doesn't bog you down. Applying the lessons we've learned to your approach won't guarantee a successful partnership, but it will help you ensure that you're moving in the right direction.

FUNDING YOUR BUSINESS

When It Comes to Fundraising, Speed Is Everything

Raising capital is often a stressful, time-consuming process for entrepreneurs. In this market, it seems as though you have to kiss a bunch of frogs before you find the right investment partner for your business. While going through this process, however, it's important to be mindful of timing.

When it comes to raising money, speed matters. If you don't move fast enough, you risk losing momentum as well as committed investors. Worse yet, the longer you let your round linger in the market, the more you inject unwanted complexity into the process. If you want a smooth, relatively painless capital raise, be sure to move quickly.

Momentum Matters

I've gone through three fundraising rounds at BodeTree, and each time, momentum played a key role in our success. If one wanted to take a cynical view, it would be easy to claim that there is a herd mentality in investing. Investors flock to opportunities that are in high demand and shy away from deals that seem to be languishing.

Speed is key to maintaining momentum in a capital raise. A domino effect of sorts comes into play when investors commit to participating. I don't know whether it's a fear of missing out or something else, but when one large investor commits, it seems as though everyone else falls in line in short order. That was certainly the case in the first two rounds we completed at BodeTree.

Investors Have Short Attention Spans

Our latest round, however, was a bit different. In the past, we've looked to high-net-worth individuals and highly focused institutional investors. This time, we set our sights on a group of more industry-specific strategic investors. The idea behind this move was to find partners who were uniquely positioned to help us execute in our bank-focused channel and support our growth.

The trouble with these unique organizations, unfortunately, is that their due diligence process tends to be longer and more arduous than normal. We allowed the process to drag on for months as they debated the nuance of legal language and other details. During this process, however, our existing investors, who have been highly supportive throughout our history, grew restless. Months had passed since they agreed to invest, and as time dragged on, other opportunities caught their attention.

While most of our existing investors still honored their commitments, a few dropped off due to illness, external liquidity issues, or other opportunities that popped up. I learned that investors have short attention spans and that it's important to lock them down quickly after they commit.

THE LONGER IT TAKES, THE MORE COMPLEX IT BECOMES

The last, and perhaps most significant, reason why it's important for entrepreneurs to move quickly when raising capital is that investment rounds tend to grow in complexity the longer they linger in the market. Potential investors who come in late in the game often want to explore various protections, preferences, or amendments to the operating agreement. This is expected behavior, of course, but it often causes the complexity of the deal to spiral out of control.

The reason for this exponential growth in complexity is that all the investors in a given round generally have to agree to the same set of terms. Certainly, investors can have different classes of stock or member interests, but ultimately everyone has to subscribe to the same operating agreement.

As potential investors go back and forth and drag out the process, entrepreneurs can find themselves in the unfortunate situation of having to constantly adjust things with earlier investors. This can lead to decision fatigue and, ultimately, the loss of early commitments.

Ultimately, the key is to move swiftly and with purpose when raising money. The prospect of fresh capital or new strategic support can tempt entrepreneurs into letting rounds linger in the market, but generally, the risks outweigh the potential benefits. Always remember that speed matters. Move as quickly as you can to secure commitments and move forward to funding. If you don't, you might find yourself encountering setbacks that are difficult to overcome.

Think Twice before Pushing for a Higher Valuation

I began my career in the field of business valuation, working with established companies and start-ups alike. Valuations were always approached from a technical perspective, and it was easy to make fun of founders or executives who had an absurd idea of how much their company was worth.

For my team and me, it always came down to the present value of the company's future cash flows. Sure, there were always other things to take into consideration, but ultimately the basic formula was pretty simple. If the math didn't work out, your valuation wasn't reasonable.

Of course, valuation is more of an art than a science, especially when it comes to start-ups. The future cash flows of the business can be incredibly difficult to forecast with any accuracy, and, as a result, founders and investors alike have to take a broad view of what constitutes value. Forecasted cash flows play a role, but other factors, such as early user traction, market reception, and past fundraising, can have an outsize effect on the ultimate valuation of a business.

Resist the Temptation to Overvalue Your Business

As a founder, you have to balance the needs of various investors, the desire to maintain a degree of control, and the realities of the market in which you operate. The temptation to push the value of the company to its limit can be strong. After all, a lofty valuation is a sign of a successful concept and robust investor interest. However, I've come to the conclusion that there are often unintended consequences associated with pushing for a high valuation for your business.

I've been guilty of walking this line in the past. When we raised our last investment round in 2014, we pushed toward the higher end of our value range. The reasoning was simple: we saw fantastic traction in the market, and our anticipated revenue looked strong. While we were still in a reasonable range for a business of our size, there was room for us to be more conservative.

DON'T LIMIT YOUR EXIT OPPORTUNITIES

Over the course of 2015, we attracted serious attention from two potential acquirers. Each brought a different perspective to the conversation, and I remain convinced that both would have been a solid fit for BodeTree. Over the course of our discussions, however, the topic of valuation came up repeatedly. For these acquirers, historical revenue, not anticipated revenue, was the benchmark of value.

As a result, their cash flow–based assessment differed from our strategic valuation. This difference in valuation perspectives made things difficult. After all, the investors who joined us in our most recent round wouldn't accept a sale price that was lower than their investment price.

Ultimately, we were unable to reach a deal in either instance. Would we have been able to had we accepted a more conservative valuation earlier on? It's difficult to say, but I suspect it would have helped.

AVOID THE VALUATION ESCALATOR

Fortunately for BodeTree, our issues have simply been a matter of timing. Once our revenue began to catch up with our expectations, our valuation became much more reasonable in the marketplace. We're currently raising another round of capital to fuel our growth, and that introduces another potential pitfall: the valuation escalator.

It's a matter of human nature to double down when things are going well. Businesses tend to jump on the valuation escalator when embarking on subsequent investment rounds. Now that our revenue has started to catch up with our previous valuation, we're facing the temptation to push it even further. This time, however, we've resisted the temptation and are seeking a "follow-on round" at the same valuation as our last round.

The reasoning for this approach is simple. By avoiding the valuation escalator, we are better positioned to take advantage of strategic opportunities we encounter in the future. Even better, our revenue growth and solid foundation put us on track for higher, yet more sustainable valuations in the future.

My advice to entrepreneurs: Think long and hard about what accepting a high valuation might mean for your start-up. While a big number may be a flattering indicator of your success so far, it could also limit your opportunities in the near term.

HOW TO RAISE MONEY IN UNCERTAIN TIMES

We live in an age of miracle and wonder, in which the pace of innovation seems to be ever-accelerating toward an increasingly connected future. However, the path forward is anything but smooth. If often feels as if the only certainty in this world is uncertainty itself. Oil prices remain artificially low, global equity markets continue to show high volatility, the IPO market has dried up, and many of the once unassailable private unicorn companies are beginning to wobble.

All these economic factors may seem abstract, but in reality their very existence is likely to pose problems for entrepreneurs of all sizes in the near term. The perception of market uncertainty spreads like wildfire, affecting angel investors and institutional venture firms alike. The capital markets for start-ups and small businesses are poised to dry up in the coming months, and smart entrepreneurs need to act now in order to survive the drought. To borrow a line from *Game of Thrones*, the investment winter is coming: now is the time to prepare.

GET STARTED NOW

Start-up investing is unique in that the positions investors take are highly illiquid and speculative. After all, when you're investing in an early-stage business, you're really taking a bet on the management team and potential for a tremendous exit at some point in the future. Start-up investing is often emotional investing, and that causes the pendulum to swing to extremes overnight. When times are good, capital flows freely. When times change for the worse, however, capital can dry up overnight. Entrepreneurs need to recognize that the winds are constantly shifting and that the capital environment of the future is likely to look unlike anything we've seen before.

Start-ups and small businesses looking to raise capital shouldn't wait to see how things play out. Entrepreneurs with strong businesses will survive prolonged periods of uncertainty, but in order to do so, they need to make sure that they have plenty of cash in reserve for the coming "funding winter."

LOOK TO EXISTING INVESTORS FOR SUPPORT

So how should an entrepreneur go about getting started? The best strategy is always to start with your existing investors. After all, they've already committed their capital and effort to the business you've created and have a vested interest in protecting their investment. More often than not, existing investors "keep their powder dry" for future rounds and are willing to participate when asked to maintain their pro rata ownership or increase their position.

Even investors who choose not to participate in a new round can still be a tremendous help. Ask for introductions to other investors in their network or for advice on how to move forward. Many times, the old adage— "ask for money, and get advice; ask for advice, and get money"—holds true. Never underestimate the power of the personal network and the fear of missing out. These two powerful drivers are vital to successful capital raising.

DON'T GET GREEDY WHEN IT COMES TO VALUATION

As I've mentioned, many fledgling entrepreneurs push too hard when it comes to valuation and end up shooting themselves in the foot. Pushing for ever-increasing valuations helps to prevent dilution of early shareholders, but it also turns away new investors and limits exit options. There was a time when start-ups could get away with murder when it came to setting the value of a round. That time, however, is long gone.

I've raised a lot of capital over the course of my career. Each time, we faced the temptation to jump on the old valuation escalator, but every time, we managed to resist its seductive pull. In BodeTree's most recent round, for example, we opted to keep our round flat with our last valuation. The rationale for this was simple.

First, it protects our existing investors, who have been very supportive throughout our journey. Second, it enabled us to set a benchmark that we will be able to execute against and exceed expectations. We're realistic and open about our performance, and this transparency and humility continue to earn us the ongoing support of our backers.

I firmly believe that the investment winter is coming. It's only a matter of time until the instability of the global economy filters down to Main Street and the scrappy entrepreneurs who are trying to carve out their place in the world. Now is the time to raise capital, control expenses, and execute relentlessly against your strategy. Seek out the support of your existing investors, and don't get greedy. If I'm right, and the market does begin to dry up, the prudent and savvy companies will be the ones that survive and thrive.

NAVIGATING THE VENTURE-CAPITAL LANDSCAPE

Raising capital is a confusing, difficult, and stressful process in which logic doesn't always reign supreme. It's incredibly important for start-ups and entrepreneurs to develop an understanding of the venture-capital landscape in order to safely navigate through the process. I've done it several times throughout my career, and I've found that there is still a significant void in the investment industry.

Despite all the talk about excess capital in the tech investment sector, many young but growing companies find themselves in a metaphorical venture-capital no man's land.

Over the past few years, I have spoken to more investment firms than I can count, and most of their investment criteria are nearly identical. They want a minimum check size of at least $5 million, or around $5–10 million in annual revenue, and they can't (or won't) invest any amount below their criteria.

When I think back to BodeTree's earlier days, these investment criteria prevented us from working with many mainstream investment groups. Back then, our capital needs were significantly less than $5 million, and we had yet to turn on revenue. The response of venture-capital firms frustrated me until I recognized a trend—more and more venture-capital firms are acting like private-equity businesses these days, seeking to back established concepts that already have significant revenue. This is a totally understandable strategy, but it isn't all that helpful for a large number of start-ups that are more than an idea but that are not yet generating significant revenue.

The logical next step for most entrepreneurs who find themselves in this situation is to seek out angel investors, but that is often easier said than done. Many angels are hesitant to invest in companies that are past the seed stage but that haven't seen the explosive growth that would merit interest from venture-capital or private-equity firms. This is often because companies that have a product that are seeking a second round of investment will raise at a higher valuation than many angels are comfortable with.

So what is a company in this position supposed to do? It's difficult to say—the right answers tend to vary from company to company. However, we managed to develop a strategy that helped us successfully raise early capital and that laid the foundation for the success we're seeing today.

BROADEN YOUR GEOGRAPHIC SEARCH

While Silicon Valley and New York City are hubs of investment activity, there are plenty of investors and opportunities in other geographic regions. While you might not get the same level of validation or support that comes with an investment from a firm like Accel, you stand a better chance of securing the incremental capital you're looking for.

Additionally, there are plenty of firms that don't traditionally specialize in technology but that are looking to diversify their portfolios. We found our lead investors in Denver, Colorado, and they've become an invaluable part of our team.

REACH OUT TO POTENTIAL PARTNERS

If your company is looking to partner with large established players, consider approaching those organizations for investments. Many times you'll find that a compelling case for partnership is also a compelling argument for investing. Having partners who are also investors can help ensure commitment to the long-term success of the venture and help you "punch above your weight."

ASK FOR MORE INTRODUCTIONS, EVEN WHEN YOU'RE TURNED DOWN

This strategy seems simple, but you'd be amazed at how effective it can be. Many times when an individual or firm chooses to pass on investing in a round, it isn't out of dislike for your business but because the opportunity simply doesn't fit certain investment criteria. If you tell your story well and manage to connect with potential investors on a personal level, they're usually willing to introduce you to other individuals or firms who are a better fit.

There's never going to be a magic formula for raising capital. Everyone's story is different and has to be evaluated accordingly. However, if your company finds itself in the middling position of having a completed product and being on the cusp of significant traction, don't give up hope—there are plenty of opportunities in the market. Good companies and good ideas will get funded; it's just a matter of getting in front of a diversity of investors and being open to unique opportunities. These strategies worked for us, and I'm confident that they'll work for countless other businesses.

WHAT TO LOOK FOR IN A VENTURE-CAPITAL PARTNER

The ability to attract the attention and support of a venture-capital firm is a badge of honor for most entrepreneurs. The allure of an influx of capital and the prestige that goes along with it can be quite strong, and it often puts entrepreneurs in the position of trying to convince potential VC partners of their viability and merit. But can that actually be a mistake?

Here's the thing I've learned about real venture capital: if you have to go out of your way to convince VC investors that your business is worthy of their attention, you probably aren't ready for their capital.

By the time your business is truly ready to partner with a VC firm, you'll likely have the ability to be somewhat picky about with whom you choose to work. Finding the right VC firm for your business is imperative. Here's what I've learned to look for in potential investment partners.

UNIQUE KNOWLEDGE OF YOUR INDUSTRY

There are two types of investment capital out there: dumb money and smart money. Dumb money isn't meant to be a pejorative term. Instead, it simply refers to the type of investment capital that isn't necessarily industry-specific. With dumb money, investors are betting on the track record, personality, and experience of the entrepreneur without taking into consideration special knowledge about the industry in which the business is operating. Early-stage friends and family rounds generally fall into this category. This type of investment is high-risk, takes place at a lower valuation, and provides entrepreneurs with the runway they need to get started.

Smart money, on the other hand, comes into play later in the game. Smart money represents the kind of capital that also brings unique industry knowledge and experience to the table. BodeTree, for example, operates in the small-business and banking industries. Many of our investors either are former bankers or have strong ties to that industry, bringing a unique perspective on what it takes to succeed in that space.

For entrepreneurs, these smart money investors are incredibly valuable, because they bring a specific and often seasoned insight to your operations. If you have the choice, always choose smart money over dumb money. It might be harder to find, and it might cost a bit more, but it's almost always worth it.

ABILITY TO MAKE HIGH-LEVEL INTRODUCTIONS

Business is all about making the right connections. Whether it's a matter of attracting new talent, advisers, or customers, knowing the right people dramatically increases your chances of success. A good VC partner will be able to help you make these connections and get the most out of them. Again, it comes back to industry knowledge—if you're a fintech company, it's important that your investors have connections to banks, payment companies and other core technology organizations.

At BodeTree, our strategy revolves around serving small businesses through sales agreements with institutional partners. This provides us tremendous access to the customer base we want to serve, but it isn't without its challenges. It's difficult for a young, growing company to find a way into large, established partner organizations. While we've made excellent headway on our own recently, we owe our early wins to the introductions made on behalf of our investors. That's why it's so important to think of your investors as extensions of your team, using their knowledge and connections to thrive.

STRONG CULTURAL FIT

Perhaps the most important thing to look for in a venture-capital partner is the cultural fit. When you raise significant venture capital, it's likely that you'll give up a significant portion of your company's equity in the transaction. In doing so, you're giving up more than ownership; you're giving up a portion of your company's soul.

With ownership comes influence, and that influence cannot be misaligned with the culture that you've worked to create. For example, if you're a relatively conservative organization, you'll struggle under the influence of a more freewheeling investment partner who pushes for a different type of work environment. Similarly, if your organization has a long sales cycle, friction will develop if your investors are used to a faster, more aggressive model.

I've been extremely fortunate to have found the right partners for our long-term success. All of our investors and partners share our perspective on both the industry and the culture we want to cultivate. As we grow, however, it will be important that we remain mindful of this and continue to seek out harmonious partners. Like many others in our situation, we have a number of great opportunities ahead of us.

The key will be to keep a level head throughout the fundraising process and remain mindful of the values we hold dear. As with most things in life, successful venture-capital investment is a two-way street. For the relationship to work there has to be strong alignment between both parties.

SOMETIMES, RAISING TOO MUCH MONEY CAN COST YOU

For most tech entrepreneurs, raising money is a lot like voting in Chicago: you want to do it early and often. Common wisdom holds that you can never bring in too much and that more money means more opportunity. While there are elements of truth here, I believe that raising too much money can be catastrophic for a business, both in the near term and in the future.

PERFORMANCE PRESSURE

I've said it before, and I'll say it again—running a business is hard. It's even harder when you have the added pressure to perform on someone else's timeline. Raising a large round at a high valuation commits you to delivering even more growth in the near term in order to justify the value. While it may be possible for some organizations to accomplish this responsibly, more often than not it drives companies to pursue this near-term growth to the detriment of your long-term goals.

At BodeTree, we had the opportunity to raise significantly more capital in our last round than we ultimately did. Looking back, I'm glad we made the decision to aim lower. It's likely that we would not have been able to remain focused on our long-term vision while scrambling to deliver on near-term expectations. We felt strongly that giving ourselves the room to do what was right for the company—and avoid the pressure to grow at all costs—was the best path. And today we have no regrets.

BURN RATE

A great philosopher once said, "Mo' money, mo' problems," and I wholeheartedly agree. There's a tendency for start-up spending to rise to the maximum that its funding allows. Unfortunately, a lot of this spending is in the form of overly rich salaries, frivolous perks, and risky gambles.

A great example of this is the demise of Fab.com, a company once valued at nearly $1 billion. Fab raised about $336 million and burned through $200 million over the course of two years. It burned through all that cash without having a sustainable business model in place, pursuing risky strategies such as shifting from flash sales to holding inventory in the pursuit of near-term hypergrowth. Its managers were so willing to spend because they had so much money to spend. Without capital constraints, every idea looks like something worthy of funding, and that is a dangerous situation for any business.

I've found that having reasonable capital constraints in place can force you to put more thought into significant expenditures. At BodeTree, we've had plenty of situations where strong internal debate over competing initiatives has resulted in new conclusions and better strategies. This also ensures that once the decision has been made, the entire team backs the winner—and so we avoid the internal battles that plague competing initiatives.

DIFFICULT EXITS

At the end of the day, entrepreneurs are in the business of providing a reasonable return for their shareholders. For most, the mechanism that drives that return is a sale of the business. However, this can become almost impossible if you've raised too much money. After all, the sale price of the business must exceed the valuation that you raised in order to provide a return for later shareholders.

Seeking higher and higher funding rounds and valuations simply force the management team to double down on the hope of an IPO or mega-acquisition. Most traditional acquirers are priced out of the market, limiting the founders' options for a reasonable exit.

Opting for a conservative valuation during our last funding round at BodeTree allowed us to keep our options open and provide a clearer path to providing a decent return for our investors. Had we raised too much money and had too high of a valuation, we would have found ourselves less poised for success.

MANAGING YOUR PEOPLE

HOW TO TRAIN YOUR TEAM

For any growing business, hiring is always a process that must remain at top of mind. There's no doubt that hiring the right person from the onset is immensely important, but many overlook the effect that training has on the long-term success of any new employee.

Training is one of those things most entrepreneurs don't pay much attention to during the early days of the business. After all, you and your key team members are too busy creating a product, process, and culture on the fly to institute a formal training program.

It's only after your hard work begins to pay off and the business begins to scale that the need for a formalized approach to training all of your new hires becomes acute. I experienced this firsthand earlier this year, when it became clear that our team needed to expand significantly to keep up with increasing customer demand.

Initially, my team and I dove right into the process of getting new hires up to speed on our immediate needs. Often we paid very little attention to helping the new team members understand the larger initiatives at play. Naturally, this approach led to problems. Our new hires were confused about the bigger purpose behind their work, and the established executive team grew frustrated with projects that were misaligned to their needs and expectations.

In order to successfully navigate this period of rapid growth, we had to change. We needed a framework that was flexible, robust, and quickly implemented. To solve for this, my team and I developed a three-step process for onboarding and training new hires.

START WITH CULTURE

The level of skill that someone brings to the table is incredibly important, but it isn't necessarily what makes someone successful. Specific skills can be learned and honed over time, but the need to mesh with a company's culture comes up almost immediately. That's why we spend the first few weeks on the job helping new hires acclimate to the culture that makes our company unique.

Rather than force someone to sit through a presentation about mission and values, we try to have new hires experience them firsthand. They spend time with our customers, partners, and founding team. During this time, we reinforce the idea that we want to work with people we trust, respect, and admire—setting the stage for long-term success.

Assign a Mentor

Team members get a mentor who is tasked with making them successful. This way, we're able to foster strong relationships across the organization and create an environment where people are invested in one another's success. Mentors are responsible for not only tactical training but also long-term career development.

When it comes to assigning a mentor, we often try to pair up employees who have had minor conflicts in the past. It seems somewhat counterintuitive, but I've found that if a leader has a problem with another team member, the best thing is to create a situation in which each person is forced to make the other successful. More often than not, this structure resolves any existing conflict and forms a much stronger bond over time. This process of setting aside issues and moving forward positively helps create a much more balanced, open, and successful team at all levels.

Follow Up Early and Often

Finally, we follow up with new additions to the team early on and continue meeting on a frequent basis thereafter. This high-touch approach ensures that no one ever gets too far off course at any point in time.

I personally set aside a scheduled time each week for an open conversation with each of my direct reports and require them to do the same with theirs. These follow-up sessions don't have to be time-consuming. Often, they happen while making a coffee run or over lunch. The important thing is that we never allow problems and questions to fester. By being insanely proactive in this manner, we're able to make sure people receive the feedback and support they need exactly when they need it.

Your company's training process doesn't have to be highly structured or complicated. Instead, try creating a framework that evolves organically from your culture and that is flexible enough to work with any new addition to your team. If you ensure that your new hires understand the company's culture, are partnered with mentors who are deeply invested in their success, and have frequent opportunities for feedback, you'll find that you'll develop a more balanced and successful team.

HOW TO BRING PROBLEMS TO YOUR BOSS

One of the most valuable career skills anyone can master is the art of bringing a problem to the attention of a boss. In most cases, people handle this situation so poorly that they end up looking defensive, desperate, or disparaging.

I learned a lot about how to handle problems and bring them to the attention of leadership when I worked at a Fortune 500 company. However, I didn't master the process until I found myself on the other side of the equation. Once I started BodeTree and had a team of my own, I gained a fresh perspective. I've boiled my learnings down three key principles.

BRING SOLUTIONS, NOT PROBLEMS

The most common mistake people make when telling someone else about a problem is also the most obvious. They tend to focus on the problem rather than the solution. Instead, I've learned that team members who lead with a solution tend to be more successful. By leading with a solution, the problem is made evident and the conversation can begin from a place of positivity and action.

I experienced this firsthand over two years ago when my chief operating officer came to me with a radical idea to revamp our system from the ground up. Historically, we relied on data from the QuickBooks platform to power our platform, and this was often a challenge, because very few of the small businesses we wanted to serve actually had clean, organized accounting. What he was proposing was a fundamental shift to live, bank-transaction data instead.

He could have come to me and complained that customer adoption was lagging and pointed the finger at any number of different culprits. Instead, he formulated a solution that not only highlighted the problem but also offered a bold and proactive approach to resolving it. Immediately, I found that I was more receptive to the idea and more willing to take action.

ACCEPT RESPONSIBILITY

The absolute worst mistake that people make when bringing a problem to their boss's attention is when they fail to take on the mantle of responsibility. Whether it's acknowledging their role in causing a problem or taking responsibility for a proposed solution, people need to ensure that they're personally invested in the matter at hand.

When my COO brought me his proposed shift to live bank data, he also took responsibility for the idea. He acknowledged the potential pitfalls that we could encounter and took it on himself to help us safely navigate around those issues. He didn't come to me with complaints or even just ideas. Instead, he came with a fully fleshed-out solution and took responsibility for its implementation. That gave me a high degree of confidence in his plan and helped rally the team behind its implementation.

DON'T THINK IN ABSOLUTES

Sometimes when people bring problems to me, they get so engrossed in the problem that they fail to be intellectually honest. Very few problems in life are black or white, yet it is human nature to frame things in absolutes.

When people think in absolutes and lock into position, they set themselves up for conflict. I had a former employee who simply could not accept our firm's position on serving a particular market segment. Using absolute statements like "this will fail" and "we're heading in the wrong direction" to frame the issue resulted in frustrating confrontations rather than honest discussions. This type of black-and-white approach to our business model ultimately led to our parting ways, but it taught me an important lesson about the type of personalities that would help the company thrive (and those that would hold us back).

Bringing problems to your boss's attention is more of an art than a science. However, by bringing solutions, accepting responsibility, and remaining open-minded, you improve your odds of success.

HUMOR MATTERS WHEN HIRING

No matter how much experience you have, interviewing potential new hires is hard. Assessing a baseline level of skill or intelligence isn't that tough—it's determining the intangible "cultural fit" aspect that is so difficult. After all, how well can you really get to know people when they're on their best behavior and you're conducting an interview?

There are, of course, countless strategies and clever questions that you can employ to try to get a feel for the true nature of the person you're interviewing, but I've never had much luck with them. Instead, I've learned to look for a single trait that tells me whether a person is going to be a good fit: a sense of humor.

Humor may seem like a strange thing to look for when hiring, but I've found that it is an excellent indicator of a person's intelligence, confidence, and overall temperament. Over the years, the people who can laugh and learn are those who have succeeded at BodeTree.

HUMOR REQUIRES INTELLIGENCE AND SELF-AWARENESS

I've always thought that there is something somewhat melancholy about funny people. It is almost as though you have to possess the ability to see the world as it is, tragic flaws and all, in order to make light of it. It is that behind-the-scenes process that interests me and that gives me a glimpse into the mind of a potential team member.

After all, it is the lethal combination of intelligence and self-awareness that I'm looking for when hiring. People who can quickly digest a situation and simultaneously reflect on their thoughts, beliefs, and actions are invaluable inside of organizations. Humor, particularly self-deprecating humor, is a telltale sign that a person possesses the skills I'm looking to cultivate.

HUMOR AND EMPATHY GO HAND IN HAND

Just to be clear, I'm not looking for a standup routine in an interview. Rather, it is the ability to seek out common ground and connect with another individual that I'm interested in seeing. When someone seems to come across as effortlessly funny and relatable, it's because he or she is demonstrating a form of empathy.

Leaders need to walk a very fine line here. There is a huge difference between emotional intelligence and pandering. If a candidate were to come in and slip in a joke about your alma mater's rival school simply because he or she looked at your profile on LinkedIn, that would be pandering—and it should be dismissed.

Instead, you want to look for someone who can read a room and find ways to connect on a personal level. The ability to quickly connect with and reassure others is vital to working with clients, prospects, and fellow team members.

HUMOR HELPS DEFUSE STRESSFUL SITUATIONS

Finally, I've found that people who have a sense of humor manage stress much more effectively than their more dour counterparts do. It doesn't matter whether you're joining a start-up or a Fortune 500 company—stressful situations will arise.

As a leader, you want to find people who can keep things in perspective and not crumble under pressure. The best team members are those who can accept a situation and respond with a type of gallows humor that instantly defuses the situation.

Take Benjamin Franklin, for example. After signing the Declaration of Independence and effectively marking himself as a traitor in the eyes of the most powerful nation on earth, Franklin quipped to his fellow signers, "We must all hang together, or assuredly we shall all hang separately." While this might not have calmed the fears of everyone in attendance, it's easy to imagine that the comment brought a sense of levity to a serious and surely nerve-racking situation. That same breath of fresh air is exactly what today's overstressed teams need when faced with tough situations.

When it comes to humor, there is often more depth than meets the eye. The ability to make another person laugh or feel at ease demonstrates intelligence, self-awareness, and empathy. Leaders looking to add new team members should pay attention and recognize the positive traits hidden behind a candidate's well-timed quip. The candidate who makes you chuckle might just end up being the person you're looking to hire.

CREATING WEALTH FOR YOUR TEAM

It's no secret that part of the allure of working at a start-up is the opportunity to build up an equity position in a company with tremendous upside. It's this ownership mentality that drives start-up employees to work harder, longer, and smarter than their corporate counterparts. When everyone is an owner, teams can move mountains.

That said, dealing with start-up equity grants can be dangerous. Not every employee grasps the value of equity, and not every start-up is a path to quick millions. Overall, it's easier to get the equity portion of start-up employee compensation wrong than it is to get it right.

Now that my company, BodeTree, is starting to scale rapidly, I've had to spend more time thinking about equity plans for our team members and what this means for the organization. Throughout my process, I've come to a few key conclusions that I believe will be valuable to any entrepreneur grappling with the topic of equity participation.

THE BEST THING A LEADER CAN DO IS CREATE WEALTH FOR OTHERS

When you're a small company, every member of the team is additive. When you're a company of five, ten, or even twenty, every interaction and decision affects the culture of the firm and, ultimately, its future. As a result, the performance expectations for early employees are incredibly high.

When you couple these often-difficult performance benchmarks with the fact that any equity grant dilutes the ownership of the founders and investors, it becomes easy to see why leaders tend to be stingy with options. However, I believe that the ability to cultivate a high-performing team and willingly share equity is a hallmark of mature leadership.

One of my mentors (who happens to be a board member here at BodeTree) was, until recently, the CFO of a major national wireless carrier and has enjoyed a long and varied career. When I asked him about what career achievement he is most proud of, he described an occasion when a custodian from one of his former workplaces thanked him for the work he had done in preparing the company's employee stock ownership plan.

That plan, and the company's subsequent IPO, enabled the custodian to put all his children through college, which until that time had seemed like an unattainable dream.

My mentor's response resonated with me on a personal level and helped me realize the power that equity participation can have to transform the lives of our team members. This realization inspired me to think more deeply about how my organization handles equity compensation and to strive to create wealth for the team.

BEWARE COMPANIES THAT HAND OUT OPTIONS TOO FREELY

Despite their ability to change the lives of employees for the better, I've learned that options should still be subjected to a healthy level of skepticism and scrutiny. Companies that hand out options too freely, or in lieu of reasonable cash compensation, are likely in dire straits or woefully naive.

One thing I've learned about employee compensation is that you always have to have room for people to grow. It doesn't matter whether you're dealing with your newest intern or a key executive. As soon as people feel as if there is no room to grow and earn more, they stagnate. Founders who give away too many options early box themselves into a corner, so to speak. Without room to expand and grant more down the road, they inadvertently deincentivize their team members, leading to problems in the long term.

Leaders and team members should approach the topic of equity compensation with the seriousness and understanding that it deserves. Stock options or other forms of equity compensation represent a bond of trust, especially at small start-up firms. There must be equal buy-in on both sides of the equation, and leaders should always be sure to keep their powder dry so that they keep employees motivated and optimistic about the future.

BALANCE IS KEY

As with most things in life, the best approach when dealing with equity compensation is a balanced one. For leaders, it's important to be generous without being egregious or stupid. For employees, the key is to find a balance between immediate cash compensation and the potential for a long-term upside.

At the end of the day, nothing beats a well-thought-out and documented equity compensation plan that takes all these factors into consideration. There are no do-overs when it comes to sharing the equity of your business, so make sure you do everything in your power to get it right the first time.

How to Deal with Irrational People

In business, you get to interact with many personality types. Some people are characterized by ambition, while others are motivated by a higher calling to make a difference in the world.

I've found that more often than not, if you can identify what drives an individual on a personal level, you can find a way to work with him or her to achieve your goals. However, we've all been in situations in which this doesn't hold true. Sometimes people's behavior doesn't seem to be motivated by identifiable, logical thought. Sometimes people are simply irrational.

Learning to deal with irrational people is a particularly important skill for entrepreneurs and leaders, as challenging behavior has a tendency to manifest itself along the entrepreneurial journey. While managing such behavior isn't easy, it can be done. When it comes to dealing with difficult personalities and irrational behavior, three simple lessons stand out.

Be Empathetic

First and foremost, it's important to stop and recognize that everyone, including you, can act irrational and crazy at times. Many factors influence our behavior in tense situations, and more often than not, people on the other side of the table are privy only to the most obvious.

Personal issues, private stresses, and unseen anxieties influence our behavior. The most important step to successfully manage someone who is acting irrationally is to start with empathy.

An empathetic response can instantly defuse a rapidly escalating situation. Begin by recognizing the other person's feelings as valid without condoning or commenting on them. The last thing that an irrational person wants to hear is that his or her beliefs or emotions are wrong. They may be misguided and factually incorrect, but they're still very real to the person experiencing them. Interactions take a turn for the worse when you push back against an irrational person, causing him or her to double down on a position and fight back.

IDENTIFY TRIGGERS

It's easy to use blanket statements and write someone off as "crazy" or "clueless," but the truth is that irrational behavior ebbs and flows. Some people may be more susceptible to it than others are, but ultimately, everyone experiences it at different points. Situational or emotional triggers in interactions often bring on irrational behavior. Learning to identify and manage these triggers is the second step to successfully dealing with tough situations.

To identify triggers in others, you must first identify the situations that trigger negative responses in your life. Self-awareness is the key to connecting with others and earning their trust. If you know that a team member or partner responds particularly poorly to something like difficulties with investors, then make sure that you carefully manage those interactions.

This doesn't mean that you should hide the truth from people. Instead, just recognize that the situation will trigger an irrational response and ease into it. Help the other person put things in context, and go into the interaction knowing that it's going to be difficult. Knowing what triggers a negative response helps you prepare ahead of time, keep your cool, and remain empathetic.

BE VULNERABLE AND TRY TO MAKE A CONNECTION

One of the worst mistakes that you can make when dealing with an irrational person is to be combative. Fighting and trying to prove that you're right in these situations is a losing battle and one that will likely result in a scorched-earth outcome. Resist the temptation to fight even when the other person is clearly in the wrong. Instead, do your best to be vulnerable and connect with the rational person on the inside.

You're not always going to win, but I've learned that you can remain strong and committed to an ideal while still being empathetic, vulnerable, and open. The ability to talk someone down from the ledge, so to speak, is a skill that every leader needs to cultivate. It all stems from sincerity and the confident belief in the value of others. Only by appealing to his or her better nature can you make a meaningful connection with an irrational person and achieve your mutual goals.

THREE QUESTIONS TO ASK EVERY CANDIDATE

I've adopted a simple rule for all hires we make at BodeTree: we hire people we trust, respect, and admire. It sounds trite, but I've found that if the candidate fits those criteria, everything from cultural fit to skills naturally falls in line.

But this is easier said than done. After all, trust, respect, and admiration are feelings that develop over time. It can be incredibly difficult to determine whether a candidate possesses these intangible values over the course of a traditional interview. The trick is asking the right questions and then reflecting on both the content and delivery of their answers. Here's how we do it at BodeTree.

Trust is at the foundation of everything we look for when hiring. It's an easy thing to look for when you're just starting to build your team. More often than not, you have already developed a strong relationship with the people you choose to be your cofounders, partners, and key executives. I was fortunate enough to have worked for my cofounder for years before we decided to start a business together.

By the time the company was founded, we had already been through good times and bad, moments of joy and periods of sheer terror. I knew that whatever came our way, I could trust him. Unfortunately, we can't always hire people we've worked with in the past. When I'm interviewing someone whom I've never met before, I say, "Tell me about a time when you stood up for your boss or coworker in front of a customer, even though you knew they were wrong."

I love this, because it provides a fascinating glimpse into the psyche of the candidate. Some people provide an example of a time when they simply lied to cover for a coworker, which calls into question the overall quality of their character. Others, however, provide examples that demonstrate decorum and composure that hint at trustworthiness. In asking this question, I'm looking for someone who can demonstrate the ability to maintain the trust of the people they work with while retaining his or her integrity.

My favorite response of all time told the story of how the candidate and her boss were in a sales meeting, lining up customers ahead of their product launch. As with any software launch, there were elements of their product that weren't fully baked yet that were in process. When her boss inadvertently committed to providing a feature that didn't fully exist, she didn't correct him. Rather, she thought on her feet, laid out an honest and reasonable path for introducing the feature, and helped the client understand why it wouldn't be available at launch. This anecdote changed my perception of the candidate and led me to believe that she was someone who would have my back while maintaining her integrity.

The level of skill that someone brings to the table is important, but it isn't the deciding factor. We've turned away plenty of rock stars in our history because they weren't necessarily people who believed in mutual respect. Skills can be learned and honed over time; respect is something that is innate. I believe that effective teamwork comes from the ground up and that dealing with outsize egos, even when they're justified by skill, simply isn't worth it. In order to begin to understand how a candidate approaches the concept of respect, I ask, "Whom do you respect the most, and why?"

When people answer this question, I've found they fall into one of two groups. The first points to a historical figure of some sort and relies on clichés. The second group points to a person they know personally and with whom they share a deep emotional bond. I'm always more interested in the second group, because their answers show that they've thought about the question before and have tried to learn from the people around them. When someone shares a story about how their parents sacrificed for them or taught them a valuable lesson, it shows me that they care deeply about respect.

Finally, we look for people who we admire. I'm a relatively young CEO, and I'm the first to admit that I don't have all the answers. That's why I surround myself with people I admire and want to emulate. I am always on the lookout for my replacement, and I urge others inside of BodeTree to do the same. Admiration is probably the most intangible and difficult to assess of the three key traits I've discussed. Here's what I say to help me begin to find out whether the candidate is someone I could admire: "Tell me about a time you failed at a goal you needed to achieve."

Failure is a universal experience, and I've found that the way a person deals with it is a great indicator of overall character. People who are unable to display a strong sense of self-awareness and humility in describing their failures are usually not admirable. I think that deep down, managers want to work with reasonable people, and if you can't be honest about your past mistakes, it's unlikely that you'll take ownership of issues that arise in the future. That's why I look for people who can recognize their mistakes, take ownership of them, and keep moving forward.

I once asked this question to a candidate who was seeking a marketing position with BodeTree, and I'll never forget his response. He told me the story of having applied at another start-up earlier in his career and being passed over. However, rather than shrug it off, he set out to understand why. Fortunately, the hiring manager was willing to share valuable feedback regarding the thought process behind his being passed over. From there, he embarked on a path to self-improvement in order to achieve his goal in the future. I was impressed by the story, because it showed a strong sense of self-awareness and a willingness to work for things he really wanted.

Perhaps I'm oversimplifying things with this approach, but it has proven successful for us so far. It's so tempting to cut corners in these areas and compromise your principles because a candidate has incredible skills or valuable connections, but in the end it is never worth it. By focusing on the fundamentals of trust, respect, and admiration, you can create a foundation for your team that allows you to overcome any challenge that comes your way.

ENLIGHTENED ENTREPRENEURSHIP

PUTTING DIVERSITY FIRST

Among the many reasons why start-ups fail, a prevailing culture of obstinacy and narrow-minded thinking is often to blame. In the male-dominated world of technology in particular, irrational commitment to a particular vision can blind founders and investors to glaring flaws in logic. To combat this, good leaders seek out a diversity of opinion in order to adjust their approach and proceed down a successful path. I've learned, however, that pursuing diverse opinions isn't enough. In order to be successful, founders need to seek out diverse perspectives.

DON'T MISTAKE DIFFERENCE OF OPINION FOR DIFFERENCE OF PERSPECTIVE

Throughout much of my company's history, we had an all-male team, even among our numerous external partners. This was unintentional, and as the CEO, I was committed to cultivating a company culture where diverse opinions were valued. Accordingly, there were many instances of team members and advisers feeling very strongly on one topic or another, having heated conversations about our strategy, product, and marketing.

However, when reflecting on these conversations, it became clear that the different opinions diverged only in terms of tactics. No matter how strongly people disagreed, deep down we were approaching challenges and decisions from the same perspective. In retrospect, it seems obvious—what do you expect when you put a bunch of technically minded and relatively young men together in a room to solve a problem? More often than not, the result is a set of ideas and solutions that largely align.

DIVERSITY HAS TO BE CULTIVATED

We set out to change this dynamic by intentionally cultivating a more diverse team across the board. This meant that we had to put diversity of perspectives at the forefront of our recruiting process while still focusing on the best-qualified candidates.

When we hired more female employees, we found that we were having far more meaningful discussions and making more impactful decisions. The cultural shift was significant and beneficial. I learned that cultivating a culture with many diverse perspectives matters if you want to develop a well-rounded product, strategy, and business.

Now when we hire, we look for candidates with perspectives that can challenge us to approach problems differently and think about our company in different ways. It just so happens that in doing so we managed to significantly improve the gender imbalance at BodeTree. Over the past few years we've shifted from a 100 percent male-dominated team to one in which about 43 percent of our staff members are female.

MATCH THE DIVERSITY OF YOUR TEAM TO THAT OF THE CUSTOMERS YOU SERVE

When we set out to bring a variety of perspectives to the business, we didn't specifically set out to hire more women. Instead, we worked to create a well-rounded culture that bore little resemblance to the Red Bull–fueled frat house start-ups with which we're unfortunately familiar.

Our goal was to match the diversity of our team with the diversity of our customer base so that every customer felt represented. By articulating our commitment to diversity up front and regularly stepping back to ensure that we were reflecting the perspectives of our customers, we found that the right candidates continually rose to the top of our list.

Our approach wasn't a matter of "affirmative action" for women or any other group; instead, we transformed our company into something that people from a variety of backgrounds wanted to be a part of. We rallied around our mission to better serve small business and our commitment to intellectual honesty, both of which subsequently attracted a unique and highly qualified set of candidates. As a result, our product has improved, our marketing has thrived, and our business has entered into a major period of growth.

Start-ups that fail to seek out diverse perspectives or hire simply for the sake of improving gender imbalance internally are making a grave error. This behavior will only perpetuate existing weaknesses and prevent the business from reaching its full potential. Approaching gender imbalance as a strategic issue and cultivating a culture in which diverse perspectives are not only tolerated but also valued will go a long way toward helping a company grow and thrive.

MANAGING OUTSOURCED EMPLOYEES

Relying on third-party contractors to sell your product or carry your brand message is not a problem unique to large operators like Uber. Small businesses and start-ups grapple with the challenge of how to work closely with partners and other types of "outsourced employees" more than they may even realize.

At BodeTree, we work very closely with partners who sell and support our system across a number of channels. In a way, these partnership channels become so-called proxy employees as they carry our product and brand message to end users. It can be daunting to manage and support teams like this, but if you're able to overcome the inherent difficulties, the benefit of such a strategy can be immense.

Over the past few years, we've learned a lot about managing these partnerships the hard way, and this experience has helped us develop real expertise in the area. Here are my top three tips for managing an outsourced team.

FULLY ALIGN YOUR INTERESTS

Structuring partnerships and signing contracts is easy for talented business development professionals, but executing on those contracts can be very difficult. In these types of relationships, you're typically dealing with multiple levels of your partner's organization. Communicating the value of your new partnership all the way down to the more tactical players is often far easier said than done. As a result, it's easy for initiatives to get bogged down moving throughout the organization during execution. Making sure that everyone who plays a part in enacting the details of your partnership understands how it serves his or her individual interests is key.

It's also imperative that your team members spend the time to get to know the key players at every level of your partner's organization who will be involved in implementation. If you learn what makes your counterparts tick, you can begin to cultivate their excitement about and understanding of the overall project. Some people merely want to have a seat at the table when it comes to making decisions, and others need to understand how success in your initiative will help further their own goals. Ultimately, it's incumbent on your team to ensure everyone's interests are aligned and moving toward the same end goal.

FOCUS ON SUPPORT

At BodeTree, we often outsource our partner's sales teams to serve as the front line in distributing our product. It's impossible (and often inappropriate) for us to manage these teams directly on a daily basis, making it difficult to ensure that the right message gets sent out on our behalf. Instead, we focus our efforts on offering robust support for those teams, providing both educational resources and ample training to make their jobs easier and their efforts more effective.

The old adage that a message has to be heard "seven times by seven ways" grossly understates the effort it takes to get a third-party team on the same page as your organization. In reality, it's a never-ending process of informing and reinforcing messages. We never shy away from in-person training, making sure we're always available for questions and coaching. We've found that the most successful partnerships develop when you can offer a support network that the outsourced team can rely on for the long term.

VIGOROUSLY DEFEND YOUR BRAND

The obvious risk of allowing another company to sell and support your product is the potential damage to your brand in the marketplace. If a partner's employee has a bad interaction with a customer, it ultimately comes back on you and your brand. After all, the customer rarely distinguishes between the product and the delivery channel.

Having responsibility for the outcome without significant control over the process seems like the definition of stress, but, while outsourcing, there is much you can do to defend your brand image.

The first and most important step is picking the right partner. Successful leaders work only with people whom they trust, respect, and admire. If a partner doesn't meet those criteria immediately, run in the other direction. But if a partner does pass this initial check and you choose to move forward, the next step is to tie your brands together. If your partner is responsible for distributing your product, make sure the entire package is cobranded so that both teams have a stake in how it's positioned.

Having some skin in the game, your partners will always think twice about how they're positioning the product, ensuring that your brand is as well protected as theirs.

Outsourcing—or anything that involves contractors for that matter—certainly isn't easy. But if you can manage to develop a deep partnership where interests are aligned, teams are supported, and your brand is well represented, you'll find that you'll be able to punch well above your weight in the marketplace. It's an approach that has served my start-up extremely well over the past few years and one that will serve as the backbone of our strategy for years to come.

The Secret to Long-Lasting Morale

As I've discussed before, I believe that business is largely a game of inches. More often than not, the wins that propel your business forward are hard won. They take time, effort, and extreme dedication on behalf of your entire team. It's easy to feel exhausted by the time you reach the finish line, but I've learned that it's incredibly important not to let the struggle get the best of you. Success is a function of your team's efforts, and you have to celebrate those efforts if you want to foster positive morale going forward.

Don't Take Wins for Granted

Our sales cycle tends to be long and challenging. It's simply the price of doing business in our industry. There are many times when we are on the verge of signing a contract only to have the timeline pushed out an additional month at the very last minute. As a result, when a deal is finally signed, it can feel somewhat anticlimactic. I've learned that as a leader, you have to fight against those feelings. If you don't, the members of your team will feel as if they're bogged down in an unwinnable battle, and morale will suffer. Every win counts, no matter how big or small—and wins should be celebrated.

Remember That People Need Constant Reinforcement

For some leaders, there's a temptation to look at victory celebrations as an unnecessary cost center. It's easy to fall into the mental trap of thinking that closing deals and moving the business forward is people's job and that their baseline compensation should be sufficient. The reality, however, is that money isn't the sole motivator for many people. It's an important part of the equation, but ultimately, great employees are motivated by intangibles.

It's the recognition of a job well done, or a sign of empathy after a long battle, that keeps people going. Regardless of the underlying logic, the truth is that people need constant reinforcement and recognition. It isn't enough just to pay people or fall back on the "it's your job" defense. Real leaders understand their team members and have empathy. This empathy allows leaders to understand what drives people and helps them to reward team members in meaningful ways.

LET YOUR CULTURE SHINE THROUGH

Not every celebration needs to be extravagant. In fact, victory celebrations are often a great chance for you to reinforce the key tenets of your company's culture and values. At BodeTree, we have a culture that values irreverent fun. I've learned that you have to have a sense of humor if you're going to stay sane in the small-business financial services space. As a result, many of our team's celebrations tend to revolve around dares or practical jokes.

BodeTree is based in Denver, Colorado, and for those who aren't aware, we have a local treasure that is both loved and reviled: Casa Bonita. Casa Bonita has been described as the "unholy lovechild of Disneyland and Tijuana" and was immortalized in a classic episode of *South Park*. It boasts indoor cliff divers, all-you-can-eat sopaipillas, and wonders such as Black Bart's Cave. In short, it's a beautiful disaster, well past its prime but still managing to hold on. When the team and I started courting a major, game-changing client, I jokingly mentioned that we would celebrate at Casa Bonita if we signed the deal.

Over the course of six months, it somehow transformed from a passing joke to a dare—to a real goal. Well, we ended up signing that transformational contract and, because I am a man of my word, we went to Casa Bonita.

It's easy to joke about, but this trip went a long way toward solidifying our team's bond, boosting morale, and cementing our corporate culture. It brought a personal sense of positivity and joy to a major business victory and humanized the whole process. I learned that you can't let victories go uncelebrated and that people need constant recognition and reinforcement that tie into your overall culture.

Sure, we worked hard to close an amazing deal—but, more important, we journeyed into the depths of Casa Bonita and emerged stronger as a team. There will be more successes in the future, and while I'm not sure we have the physical constitution to survive another trip to the Casa, you can be sure that we'll find other new ways to celebrate and strengthen the bond our team shares.

MAKING INTERNSHIPS WORK

Internships always seem to be binary experiences. For the lucky group, they mean many hours completing meaningful and enriching tasks for little to no pay, learning the art of sitting behind a desk for eight hours at a stretch, and finding out the hard way what business casual attire actually means.

For the not-so-lucky, internship season means taking anywhere from a few minutes to a few hours out of your already busy day to steer idealistic youngsters around the office while hoping that nothing gets broken.

The good news is that internship season doesn't have to be so grim. In fact, internships can provide useful and formative experiences on both sides of the desk. From my time as an admittedly insufferable finance intern to hiring interns of my own, I've gathered a handful of experiences in hopes of reshaping how others look at this professional rite of passage.

TRANSFORM THE OPPORTUNITY

I was a finance major in college and had grand ambitions to break into the world of investment banking. Unfortunately, Arizona State University wasn't a major recruitment hub, and Goldman Sachs wasn't exactly knocking on my door.

In my search for experience, I came across an Arizona-based real-estate investment trust company called Cole Capital (now part of American Realty Capital) at a summer internship fair at my university. It was somewhat related to my major, and the company seemed somewhat interested in having a conversation, which was enough to convince me to give it a try. The internship was in the back-office operations department and wasn't all that glamorous. Instead of looking at it as a disappointment, I chose to transform the opportunity.

I drew up a simple road map of what I wanted to accomplish and where I wanted to end up. I knew I wanted a full-time position that enabled me to learn about the investment-related aspects of the business, but I also wanted to gain a better overall understanding of the industry. I made sure that I completed my task list as efficiently as possible, using the extra time to take on projects that helped me gain insight into the business and work with different people within the team.

It didn't take long before I was focusing on these new projects on a full-time basis. Through this experience, I learned that the real value of an internship is the chance to be part of a team. Once I was in the door, I could define the experience for myself.

FIND A MENTOR/BE A MENTOR

During my internship experience, I was lucky enough to find two mentors who helped guide me and open new doors along the way, which proved invaluable.

The first was my immediate boss, who understood what I wanted to accomplish and helped me navigate the corporate landscape. He gave me more freedom than I deserved as an ambitious nineteen-year-old but always stood by quietly in the wings to reel me back in when I was getting ahead of myself. It was his support that made it possible for me to connect with my second mentor, the company's founder and CEO. He took the concept of mentorship to the next level, introducing me to fascinating people and experiences that I cherish to this day.

The trick to finding good mentors is simple: ask them to mentor you. Asking someone to become your mentor signals that you want to learn and that you value his or her insight and experience. Many interns I've encountered over the years take a passive approach, waiting for someone to approach them with grand opportunities. You have to take it on yourself to make things happen even if you don't know exactly what they are.

MAKE YOURSELF INDISPENSABLE

The final and most important lesson I've learned is to make yourself indispensable to the organization. As an intern, you're not going to have the most knowledge or experience. Acting like a know-it-all or coming across as overly confident will stop you dead in your tracks. Instead, make yourself indispensable to the team by having a sincere sense of humility, being the easiest to work with, and, above all, outworking everyone.

When I started at Cole, I knew nothing about real-estate investment trusts and could offer nothing of real value to the organization. I wanted the chance to learn from the team, but I couldn't expect the team members to stop what they were doing and take time out of their busy day to teach me. I had to make it worth their while to engage with me, so I took on every bit of grunt work they threw my way. I ended up doing the work of several interns. Before long, I was viewed as an indispensable part of their team, which finally made it worth their time to teach me.

When I look back on my time as an intern, I'm overwhelmingly grateful for the experience. I learned some valuable lessons—and now that I have my company, BodeTree, I aim to infuse the same opportunity into the internships at BodeTree today.

Having interns serves as a powerful reminder that we all started somewhere. Offering opportunities to those who are eager and interested enough to take them may mean a few more hours of work for you, but you could be mentoring a future start-up founder, CEO, or employee.

EXITING YOUR BUSINESS

BEWARE THESE THREE SCARY NEGOTIATION TACTICS

Negotiation can be a tricky business, full of both potential pitfalls and opportunities for success. When two parties negotiate in good faith, the results can be mutually beneficial and can fortify a relationship that is based on trust, respect, and admiration. Unfortunately, not every negotiation is in good faith.

Often, in fact, negotiating a deal is a scary and adversarial experience. Aggressive negotiators usually have some tricks up their sleeves and can use them to devastating effect. I've experienced some of these firsthand over the years and now am prepared to maneuver around the pitfalls they present.

MANIPULATING THE ENVIRONMENT TO GAIN AN ADVANTAGE

Environment plays a tremendously powerful role in determining the outcome of any negotiation. One surprisingly common tactic that I've seen repeatedly is to take whomever you're negotiating with out for drinks the night before. What may seem like a gesture of goodwill subtly becomes a late night out that leaves the other person worse for the wear when it's time to get down to business the next day.

The trick to overcoming this particular tactic is to be mindful of its existence and to plan ahead. If your client or partner wants to take you out the night before, be smart—don't drink too much. Some of the savviest businesspeople I've even encountered have perfected the art of pretending to drink. As those around them begin to let their guard down, they remain sharp. Always be mindful of your environment, and recognize that every situation you find yourself in, no matter how fun or casual, is part of the negotiation.

"NEGGING"

In the strange and often terrifying world of the pickup artist exists a tactic known as "negging"—the practice of delivering a backhanded compliment or insult designed to undermine another person's confidence, driving him or her to seek approval. The tactic is just as twisted and underhanded

ENLIGHTENED ENTREPRENEURSHIP

as it is effective. For skilled negotiators, the approach can successfully play on the insecurities, anxieties, and perceived weaknesses that everyone (particularly entrepreneurs) experiences.

I've dealt with this one quite a few times in my role as the CEO of BodeTree. When meeting with a large, publicly traded or incredibly well-capitalized organization, I'll hear comments like, "You've accomplished a lot with such a small team," or "You know how to get a lot out of limited resources." Early on, these types of comments made me defensive and desperate for the speaker's approval. I've learned, however, that everyone is susceptible to this strategy, even the people who make good use of it.

Don't be afraid to give the other person a taste of his or her own medicine. If you're a scrappy upstart going up against the established player in your industry, know your facts and fire back. In my case, a typical response of my own would include a hearty, "Thanks! I really respect how conservative and thoughtful your team has been in this space. I'm sure your stock will come to reflect the value of your approach."

CREATING DISSENSION IN YOUR CAMP

Perhaps the most insidious strategy I've come across in negotiations is the effort to sow the seeds of discord within the team across the table. This happens most often when you're dealing with a potential acquisition scenario or in any other situation where one side can cut a better deal with one person to the detriment of the rest of the team. Not too long ago, I found myself in a situation where an organization was interested in trying to acquire BodeTree at a price point that would have been unacceptable to a good number of our investors. The conversation at the negotiation table took a dark turn when the other side tried to offer me a very attractive compensation plan outside the transaction itself. Essentially, they were trying to bribe me into advocating a deal that would have been bad for my investors, bad for our customers, and bad for my team.

Successful negotiations generally require a single point person to take charge, and that is always risky. If the lead negotiator from your team encounters a moral hazard such as a side deal or promises of great things in the future, the entire dynamic of the negotiation can be thrown off. To insulate against this, make sure that your lead keeps clear lines of communication open with the board and other key stakeholders. Second, be certain that whoever is leading the negotiation has a strong moral compass and is fully invested in the well-being of the company's shareholders, customers, and team members.

Remember—not all negotiations are friendly. At some point in your career, you're going to find yourself up against an adversary who knows how to take advantage of these strategies. The key to resisting these effects is to spot them early in the process. Knowing what you're up against is half the battle, and with a little bit of preparation and a whole lot of confidence, you'll be able to fight back.

DON'T BE NAIVE

For entrepreneurs, few things are as flattering or exciting as a potential acquisition. When someone approaches you to express an interest in buying your business, it seems like the ultimate validation of your ideas, effort, and team. Unfortunately, this flattery can often cloud founders' judgment and lead to serious problems.

I've been in this position a few times now at BodeTree and have let my naïveté get the better of me on more than one occasion. Even though we've never been looking to sell, as the CEO, I have a fiduciary responsibility to my shareholders to explore legitimate opportunities that come our way. Over the years, I've learned the hard way that interest from potential acquirers isn't always what it seems.

IF IT SOUNDS TOO GOOD TO BE TRUE, IT PROBABLY IS

Acquisitions are almost always a tedious process for everyone involved. Buyers have to go through a robust due diligence process, and sellers have to deal with questions of valuation, the concerns of existing stakeholders, and near-constant uncertainty. Entrepreneurs should take note when the process seems to be moving abnormally fast or if things seem too easy. The old maxim holds true: if it sounds too good to be true, it probably is.

Once, I found myself in an early-stage meeting with a potential acquirer who got right to business discussing acquisition prices and tactical details. In my naïveté, I took this as a sign of strong interest. One of my more seasoned colleagues, however, immediately recognized it for what it was: a test. The representatives from the organization wanted to gauge my willingness and sophistication. In my excitement, I was all too willing to take those words at face value, and I allowed myself to become ensnared in a fantasy.

RECOGNIZE THAT EVERYTHING IS A BUILD-OR-BUY SCENARIO

Founders tend to overvalue the company they've built, both financially and conceptually. Having worked on both sides of the table at various points in my life, I've learned that almost every buyer approaches a transaction from the perspective of building versus buying. Simply put, anyone who expresses interest in acquiring a business must first decide whether to try to build the product, service, or revenue stream in question internally instead.

Some potential buyers are transparent and honest about this decision. However, many aren't entirely well intentioned and will use acquisition discussions as an opportunity to steal your ideas. Naive entrepreneurs will fail to recognize this possibility. Believe me—other organizations can and will try to recreate your product themselves.

DON'T GET TOO EXCITED

The allure of a business exit can be strong. After all, few other events have the potential to create lasting wealth for everyone involved. Allowing your excitement to get the better of you, however, is never a good thing. When entrepreneurs are too eager to move forward in the process, they often get distracted, make strategic mistakes, and leave money on the table. Instead, founders need to temper their excitement and remain in full control of the opportunity.

I allowed my first real acquisition opportunity to get the better of me. It was early on in BodeTree's history, and I found the prospect of combining with a much larger organization to be intoxicating. With our product and their resources, I thought that we could accomplish great things. Moreover, such a quick exit would provide an excellent return to our early investors, validating everything we were trying to do. In perhaps the ultimate sign of naïveté, I allowed this opportunity to dominate my every thought for weeks on end. The deal never materialized, and I ended up distracted from the task at hand. I learned the hard way that I had to keep cool and temper my expectations to stay on point.

For entrepreneurs and investors alike, navigating a business toward a successful exit is an important undertaking. More often than not, acquisitions by larger and more established businesses represent the quickest path to that goal. However, the acquisition process is fraught with challenges, and failing to understand the nuances and pitfalls of selling a business can lead to major problems.

My advice, most of which was learned the hard way, is simple—if an opportunity looks too good to be true, it probably is. Second, recognize that potential acquirers will always try to decide whether it makes more sense to build the product internally rather than buy it. Finally, and perhaps most important, don't let your eagerness for an exit cloud your judgment. When it comes to selling your business, don't be naive.

AN EXIT ISN'T A BAD THING

Building a business is an intensely personal endeavor. When you create something from scratch, you can't help but imbue it with your personal thoughts, feelings, and perspectives. Your business becomes an extension of your identity.

Personal investment is what drives entrepreneurs to be so passionate about their companies and products, but it can also cloud their judgment when it comes to exploring a potential exit. At BodeTree, we've had many conversations with organizations interested in acquiring the company. Over the years, I've learned how to handle these opportunities and make sure that I'm always looking out for the best interests of our organization, team members, and investors.

BE REALISTIC

The simple truth is that most entrepreneurs aren't going to become phenomenally rich and successful from their ideas. Sure, there are so-called unicorn companies that pop up every few years, raising hundreds of millions of dollars, but more often than not, new ventures either fail or reach a middling level of success. Unfortunately, although most entrepreneurs recognize this fact, most still think that their idea is the exception.

Much like playing the lottery, nearly everyone knows that the odds of winning the jackpot are insanely low, but deep down, they still think they have a better than average chance. That sort of thinking is part of human nature, but I believe that the inherent logical fallacy at play can be incredibly damaging.

Entrepreneurs must recognize that there is no shame in building a company worth $5 million, $10 million, or $20 million. Although such valuations fall short of the billions of dollars you see when dealing with unicorn companies like Uber or Slack, they still represent a tremendous value creation and the opportunity to provide a solid return for your investors. There's also a strategic element at play here.

Not every founder is well positioned to scale and grow his or her company as it matures. Many times, even more value can be created if the founder cedes power to an acquiring organization. The key is to recognize that so-called little wins are still, in fact, wins. Unrealistic expectations, either about the value of your business or your ability to execute going forward, will only limit your success.

DON'T FEAR AN EXIT

It's fashionable for founders to claim that they're "in it for the long haul" and are "looking to build a lasting enterprise." There's absolutely nothing wrong with that, and in fact it's an admirable thing to say. It's also largely untrue. Most entrepreneurs are looking to build a company that is impactful in the world and makes money. Everyone wants to change the world, but at the end of the day, you have to be able to provide a return to your investors.

Founders should always be on the lookout for a potential exit. Whether it's selling the business or just surveying the landscape, a responsible founder must always have a solid understanding of the exit options.

When entrepreneurs understand their exit opportunities, they're able to develop better overall strategies for their organizations. For most companies, there are lots of potential suitors or partners, each of which has a unique strategic implication for the future of the business.

At BodeTree, we've worked with everyone from banks to insurance companies, and each interaction has helped us understand our overall opportunity, the market's needs, and our place in it. It also helped us formulate our long-term strategy and refine our goals. When entrepreneurs refuse to engage with potential suitors out of principle, they miss out on valuable insights that can help them in the long run.

THERE ARE SECOND ACTS IN ENTREPRENEURIAL LIVES

If you're an entrepreneur, there's a very good chance that your current endeavor will not be your last. In fact, many of the most successful entrepreneurs in the world hit their stride on the second or third attempt. Take Uber CEO Travis Kalanick, for example. He founded two companies prior to starting Uber, one of which sold to Akamai Technologies for $19 million.

I have no doubt that the skills he learned in his earlier ventures and the credibility he gained with a successful exit helped propel Uber to what it is today.

The lesson here is that there are second acts in life, and it's important to remember that when running your business. Think about what the future holds and how a potential exit, even if it isn't what you had in mind, can play into your future goals.

My advice to fellow founders is to stay humble and realistic about the company you've built. There's nothing wrong with exploring potential exits or even selling your business early on. Being open to opportunities can help you improve your existing business or even set you on the path to success in a future endeavor. Clinging to unrealistic expectations and getting in your own way only limits your potential.

Dispelling the Myth That Founders Can't Scale

It's often been said that "founders can't scale," and more often than not it proves to be true. It's a familiar story: as a company grows, the founder finds him- or herself replaced by someone from a traditional management background. The reason for the replacement usually has less to do with the founder's technical ability and more to do with his or her overall leadership style.

As a company grows, the founder-centric (and often ego-driven) approach that helped get the business off the ground becomes a potential hindrance to expansion and diversification.

Successful long-term leaders exhibit a markedly different skill set than founders, one that plays down their ego and puts the needs of their company and team before their own. It's a deceptively simple concept but one that is incredibly difficult to put into practice with any consistency, especially when you're dealing with the business you founded.

The truth is that if you are going to have even a remote chance of creating and running a successful, long-lasting company, you will need trust, loyalty, and support. The only way to gain those things is to give them away. That's the very core of being a servant leader, and it's the secret to beating the "founders can't scale" curse.

Transitioning into this mature management style can be an incredibly difficult task for founders who risked everything to build their company, but it is by no means impossible. As the cofounder of BodeTree, I have had to set my own ego aside as our company has continued to grow. I don't claim to have all the answers, but here are three steps that helped me transition into servant leadership.

Always Think of Others

It's incredibly easy to get caught up in the petty details of running a company. Worries about compensation, titles, and who gets credit for what can (and often do) eat up the bulk of your day. These worries are not only pointless but also harmful and counterproductive.

When we made our first key hires, I felt excited and threatened at the same time. What if the person we hired knew more than I did? Would my opinion still carry weight? It took me longer than I like to admit to realize that these concerns were ridiculous and wildly immature. Instead of worrying, I should have been doing everything in my power to help make everyone on my team as successful as possible.

Only after I stopped fretting about myself and started worrying about my team members did I begin to earn their trust and respect. The change in attitude filled me with a newfound confidence, and the team had a renewed sense of energy and excitement.

STAY HUMBLE

It's really difficult to "sit low" and take a back seat, especially for young founders. I've always had an underlying fear that my position and authority were tenuous because of my age and relative lack of experience. This once caused me to jockey for attention and praise in an attempt to find validation. However, the more I did this, the less confident I felt.

I've since realized that two things are necessary in order to have the confidence to always put others before yourself: trust and humility. The inescapable fact is that you are never as smart, talented, or lucky as you think you are. Trying to prove otherwise is a recipe for disaster. Having the humility to recognize your own shortcomings is the path to success. This sense of humility, coupled with a team that you trust, respect, and admire, can make it possible to easily put others before yourself.

KEEP IMPROVING

Even the most dedicated servant leader will stray from the path at times. What's important is that you keep trying to get back on the right track.

One thing I've found that helps is to be totally transparent with your team about your shortcomings. People are far more patient and forgiving when they know what you're striving for and when they see you quickly admit when you're in the wrong. Even more important, you need to be patient with yourself.

A healthy ego can help a founder get started, but unless he or she learns to grow alongside the company and serve others first, it will be the stumbling block that keeps the founder from scaling.

Part 3: Staying Sane

Entrepreneurship is a taxing journey in every sense of the word. It will test you physically, financially, and emotionally. Navigating the experience while maintaining your sanity is easier said than done. However, I've found that it is possible to start and run a business without losing your mind or soul. In this section, I'll explore the following:

- how to manage yourself;
- how to find balance;
- leadership lessons; and
- how to manage anxiety and depression.

MANAGING YOURSELF

DON'T LET INSECURITY DERAIL YOU

There's a common perception of entrepreneurs as bold, brash, and exceedingly confident individuals. This belief is so common, in fact, that entrepreneurs themselves often buy into it. Fledgling founders think that they have to emulate a fictionalized Mark Zuckerberg in *The Social Network* or recreate the exploits of a young Steve Jobs in order to be taken seriously. They're taught to never show fear, to focus on their "personal brands," and to always be the smartest person in the room.

As an entrepreneur myself, I know that this is a false and damaging belief. The truth is that it's often insecurity rather than confidence that drives our actions. Deep down, we all have something to prove. We care about how the world views us and want to show our naysayers that our ideas have value.

It's our natural insecurity that drives us to push the limits and constantly reach for more. Unfortunately, when we deny the truth of our insecurity, the poor decisions that result can drive us to the brink of failure. Left unchecked, these decisions destroy not only our businesses but also our character.

THE GATEWAY TO DISHONESTY

Creating a business is one of the most difficult challenges an individual can undertake. The path of the entrepreneur is one of conflict and setbacks. At every stage of the journey, there are moments that leave you questioning yourself and the decisions you've made. With so much pressure to succeed, it's easy for entrepreneurs to fall into the habit of casual dishonesty. Whether this means inflating the number of customers you have or exaggerating your success, it usually begins innocently enough.

There is a pervasive fear among entrepreneurs that if you don't exaggerate and manipulate the truth, someone else will, and you will be left behind. Unfortunately, small lies beget larger lies. Soon, it's possible to lose track of the truth altogether.

It's difficult to compartmentalize dishonesty. Everyone tries, of course, but when you get comfortable lying in your professional life, you find that it quickly bleeds over into your personal life. Before you know it, a simple and entirely understandable insecurity leads to a snowball effect that chips away at your integrity. As I've discussed before, the truth always comes out. At the end of the day, all you have in this life is your integrity. If you allow that integrity to become compromised, the damage becomes irreparable. Customers, employees, and investors will depart, never to return.

THE PATH TO PRIDE AND ARROGANCE

Pervasive insecurity can lead even the most grounded person down the pernicious path of pride and arrogance. When insecurity takes root, the focus shifts as you constantly seek external affirmation.

This leads to an arrogance that manifests itself in different ways. Sometimes it's a cockiness that can come out when talking to potential partners; other times it's an edginess that entrepreneurs mistake for confidence. However it manifests itself, this arrogance leads to short-sighted decisions that can have long-lasting effects on the business.

Many entrepreneurs double down on their assumptions and past decisions when they're insecure. They would rather defend their egos than admit that they were wrong and alter course. I've seen this repeatedly and have been guilty of it myself in the past. This is why so many entrepreneurs choose to go down with their ship rather than listen to the advice of others. Worse yet, this arrogance leads the people around them to take silent pleasure in their inevitable failure rather than to inspire them to lend a hand in a time of need.

THE ROAD TO JEALOUSY AND ISOLATION

Finally, unchecked insecurity leads to jealousy and isolation. If you lack self-awareness, it's easy to resent the successes of people around you. When this happens, people tend to act out in subtle and often passive-aggressive ways. Sometimes it's as simple as a snide comment made in passing. Other times, it's the subconscious desire to see another's hard work amount to nothing even if that failure damages you in the process.

Ultimately, the inability to let go of your insecurities and revel in the success of others leads to isolation. Deep-seated jealousy prevents you from assisting others in reaching their goals, which is the only real job of a leader. Before you know it, no one wants to be around you, and you find yourself isolated from your team, friends, and family. No entrepreneur has ever found success entirely on his or her own. When you become isolated from those around you, it becomes almost impossible to succeed.

Everyone deals with insecurity in some form or another. Anyone who claims otherwise is simply lying. Having insecurities isn't a problem; denying those insecurities is. Entrepreneurs need to break free from the caricature of the "Jobsian" Master of the Universe and recognize their insecurities for what they are. If you don't, you'll find yourself slipping into a pattern of dishonesty, arrogance, and jealousy as you try to cope. Ultimately, these behaviors will destroy not only the business you're trying to build but also the very fabric of your character. And that, of course, is the greatest failure of all.

DEALING WITH UNCERTAINTY MAKES YOU STRONGER

Fear of the unknown is a fundamental part of human nature, a vestige of our primitive past when playing it safe was a matter of life or death. Although our society has evolved, this deeply embedded fear has remained part of the human experience.

For most of us, uncertainty in life is a constant source of anxiety, stress, and frustration. I used to think that systemic and pervasive uncertainty was unique to entrepreneurs, but now I realize that it is a challenge that faces anyone looking to play an active role in shaping the world.

Those of us who refuse to be passive players in life must contend with the stress of living with pervasive uncertainty. My family and I have dealt with it for years now, ever since I started BodeTree. It has been nearly six years of not knowing what city we'll put down roots in—six years of living on a roller coaster of emotional highs and lows.

On the surface, this may seem like a net negative experience. It's true that this sort of uncertainty often cripples people, sending them scurrying back to the safety of a less dynamic lifestyle. However, I've found that a life of uncertainty can make individuals and families stronger. As with most things in life, the more challenging path can lead to personal and professional growth.

POLISHING THE ROUGH EDGES

Throughout my life, certain phrases and insights have stuck with me while other lessons have faded. One such lesson came from a history teacher whose class I attended during my junior year of high school. I no longer remember the complete context of the conversation, but I will never forget the lesson she shared.

She spoke about how our personalities are like rough-hewn rocks—full of sharp edges and imperfections—that have been tossed into a river. Just as rocks are slowly polished and smoothed by the constant flow of the river, our personalities are polished and refined by the constant flow of challenges and uncertainty with which we contend.

CONFRONTING THE WORST ASPECTS OF YOUR PERSONALITY

That image has always stuck with me and helped me recognize the underlying value of the challenges I face. Uncertainty tends to bring out the worst parts of your personality. On a personal level, I know that my type A tendencies and anxiety often get the better of me.

The uncertainty of the entrepreneurial life has pushed these flaws out into the open and forced me to confront them head on. This internal confrontation and introspection have helped me grow as a father, husband, and leader on some levels.

I know that I've become more compassionate, self-aware, and open with those around me. I have no doubt that this accelerated path to enlightenment, so to speak, was a direct result of having to face the challenges of our uncertain place in the world. Had I taken a more comfortable path, I know that I wouldn't have been forced to contend with these aspects of my personality as directly and would have let them fester under the surface for years.

LIVING IN THE MOMENT

Perhaps the most valuable side effect of dealing with uncertainty is the ability to live in the moment. Throughout my life, I've always been looking ahead to what is next—at the expense of the present. Looking back, I think that I've missed out on opportunities, both personally and professionally, due to my constant focus on the future.

A good example of this happened last year when I was evaluating a deep strategic partnership with a much larger company. I was so focused on trying to maximize value based on what could be that I lost sight of what we needed to do in the moment. The uncertainty of the situation took its toll on me, and ultimately, nothing came of the arrangement. I realize now that had I simply focused on the moment I was in, the outcome could have been much different.

Uncertainty is part of life for those of us who are never satisfied. If you're looking to make your mark on the world, you will have to learn to deal with the anxiety and stress of staring into the void of the unknown. The fear that you'll undoubtedly experience doesn't have to cripple you. Instead, remember the parable of the rock tossed into the river. The forces that push against you work to make you a smoother, stronger, and well-rounded person.

ENTREPRENEURSHIP HAS CHANGED ME FOR THE BETTER

Life has a way of changing all of us over time, but often the change is subtle and imperceptible. There are, however, certain accelerators that can bring about rapid and meaningful change in an individual's life. The decision to become an entrepreneur is one of those accelerators. The act of creation, of building something from nothing, fundamentally changes those involved, for better or worse.

I've been thinking about my entrepreneurial journey quite a bit lately. BodeTree has come into its own over the past two years. Our growth has taken off, our team has matured, and we're beginning to make our mark on the industry in a meaningful way. It has been a long and challenging journey, with many ups and downs along the way.

The relationship between a business and its founders is coevolutionary. My company has changed for the better over the past five years, and so have I. Here are the three most important ways that my entrepreneurial journey has improved me.

COMPASSION

A powerful quote by Ernest Hemingway has always resonated with me. When asked about the process of writing, Hemingway responded, "You have to be hurt like hell before you can write seriously." I believe that the same sentiment applies to entrepreneurship.

Deep down, I feel like you're not a true entrepreneur until you've been hurt and find a way to keep going. When you do this, you find that you emerge a far more compassionate person. I've seen plenty of hurt over my five years leading BodeTree. I've experienced disappointment, betrayal, and countless failures. Rather than make me bitter, however, these experiences have made me more compassionate toward everyone I encounter. I recognize how hard things are, how stressful they can be, and how much failure hurts.

When I see others experiencing the same pain that I went through, my heart goes out to them.

I'm currently in the middle of expanding my team, raising capital, and guiding a company through hypergrowth. A few years ago, any one of these things would have caused me to be a nervous wreck. I would have been entirely overwhelmed by my responsibilities and would have struggled to cope. Now, however, years of experience have made me dramatically more confident in my ability to welcome new challenges.

The only way to build that kind of quiet confidence is through experience and self-awareness. I've learned that moving forward in the face of adversity and overwhelming odds is the only way to develop this sort of genuine confidence. Entrepreneurship threw me into the proverbial deep end, and it was through the struggle for survival that I was able to grow.

GRIT
The final and perhaps most important trait I've developed as an entrepreneur is grit. Strength of character allows you to take a hit and just keep on going, no matter what. If it weren't for grit, I wouldn't have made it this far at BodeTree.

Before I became an entrepreneur, I struggled to move forward in the face of recurring failures. If something I worked on wasn't successful, I simply gave up and moved on to a new focus. I did not have the grit necessary to keep moving forward in the face of adversity. However, the forcing function of entrepreneurship has taught me to never give up. Had I never built BodeTree, I know I wouldn't be as gritty a person as I am today. This trait has helped me pursue my dreams in the face of adversity—and to inspire others to do the same.

I'm incredibly grateful for everything my entrepreneurial journey has taught me so far. Without taking on the challenge and dealing with the pain, I wouldn't have developed traits such as compassion, confidence, and grit. Entrepreneurs from all walks of life should be aware of the symbiotic relationship between founders and the businesses they build. If you're lucky, the relationship will change you for the better.

TAKE TIME TO RELAX AND RECHARGE

If you're like me, you might find adjusting to this excess of free time a little frustrating. After all, any disruption to a well-established routine can cause heartburn for type A personalities.

Well, fear not my fellow type A entrepreneurs. I have the solution to this pernicious problem. Over the years, I've found that the trick to making the most of free time is to approach it with a sense of purpose, putting real effort into relaxing and recharging.

UNPLUG FOR A FEW DAYS

Real relaxation is difficult to achieve, due in no small part to the constant deluge of information to which we subject ourselves. E-mail, text, Slack messages, and social media notifications fire off in regular cadence, constantly demanding our attention no matter where we are. In order to gain perspective and think clearly, you have to actively distance yourself from these distractions. The only way to accomplish this is just to unplug.

This, of course, is far easier said than done. I'll be the first to admit that I'm addicted to this never-ending flow of information. It makes me feel connected, productive, and secure. The unfortunate reality, however, is that constant connectivity provides a false sense of comfort. We often mistake connectivity for true connection and busyness for true productivity. Unplugging and going analog for a period can help reset your system and force you to be present in the current moment. This forced mindfulness can be challenging, but it's the first and most important step toward relaxing and recharging.

REDISCOVER YOUR PASSION

It's easy to forget why you started your business in the first place. After all, the demands of running an organization are often extreme and draining. Now that you've unplugged and are focused on recharging, the next step is to rediscover your passion. That sounds like a gargantuan task, but it's more manageable than you might think.

Start by going back to your initial source of inspiration for your business. For me, the idea for my company, BodeTree, came from the serendipitous moment when I was working on a financial model while reading Ronald Alexander's *Wise Mind, Open Mind*. Alexander's classic work on mindfulness and Zen Buddhism helped inspire me to bring Zen to the world of small-business finance.

I truly believe that running a business from a holistic perspective can and should be simple, easy, and enlightening. That is my passion, and it is what motivates me to drive my company forward every day. I'm revisiting *Wise Mind, Open Mind* this week just to recapture my eureka moment and experience it again.

Do a Self-Assessment

There is no lonelier job than being an entrepreneurial CEO. It's a position with no peers—only employees and shareholders. It's difficult to get honest and actionable feedback, so you have to have a strong sense of self-awareness in order to survive. Without self-awareness, it's impossible to control your reaction to the trials and tribulations that life so often presents. This is especially important for leaders, as their actions (either conscious or unconscious) set the tone for the entire organization. Doing a self-assessment of your strengths and weaknesses, as well as of what excites you or causes anxiety, is one of the most important exercises a leader can do.

The first step toward self-awareness is to recognize and be open about the things that cause stress, anxiety, and negativity in your life. This self-assessment enables you to prepare yourself and your team for the challenges and opportunities that you will face in the coming year. Remember, positivity and negativity are choices; the only trick is that you have to be self-aware enough to recognize them as such.

It sounds counterintuitive, but relaxation is hard work. For type A personalities, you have to commit to relaxing and recharging and approach it just like any other project. The first step is to unplug for a period and simply go analog. This is easier said than done, but it's necessary if you're going to escape the distractions of the status quo.

Next, take the time to rediscover your passion. Get back to your roots, remembering what inspired you to start your business in the first place. Finally, work toward self-awareness by doing a self-assessment. Consider your strengths and weaknesses, and be honest with yourself. As a leader, you have to take charge of your development, so be sure to make the most of free time, using it to your advantage.

Start-up Lessons I've Learned the Hard Way

I have a confession to make. I'm a business-book addict. It's an unhealthy relationship that drains my bank account and generally leaves me with few, if any, useful insights. Yet for some reason, I can't seem to pass through the coffee-stained aisle of my local book megastore without picking up a few of the new releases. I've even taken to strategically removing them from my bookshelf so that houseguests don't mistake me for a cliché-spouting, new-age, faux business 2.0 guru.

The funny thing is that even though I've read virtually every hot business book out there, the most important lessons I've picked up while nurturing my business from a scrappy start-up to an even scrappier—and slightly more mature—start-up were learned the old-fashioned way: by living and learning.

I submit to you the top three start-up lessons that I learned the hard way.

Focus on the Pain Points

Don't roll your eyes. This lesson isn't as obvious as it seems. Every single founder thinks that his or her product solves a pain point in the market. The trouble is that not every single founder has the intellectual honesty to recognize that the pain point he or she is solving might not be big enough—or might not even be a pain point that people need to have addressed.

When we initially came up with the concept for BodeTree, the killer feature that I thought would take us to new levels of fame and fortune was our automated valuation feature. Before cofounding the company, I had been a valuation consultant and charged obscene rates to small and mid-size businesses to develop valuation reports. It wasn't uncommon to rack up a bill of $15,000 or more for a typical valuation. Now we were jumping into the market with a solution that did the same thing for fifty dollars a month. Who wouldn't fall to the ground and start praising their deity of choice for such a miraculous invention?

Lots of people, apparently. It turns out that not every owner cared about that feature as much as I did. My team and I had to put our personal biases and beliefs aside and figure out what our customers really wanted. In the end, it helped us find sustainable success by redefining the experience we provided and the customers we served.

STAY LEAN

For most start-ups, the hunt for funding can become an obsession that takes up far too much time and energy. Of course, every founder says that until he or she needs funding. BodeTree has been fortunate enough to attract media attention and traction with users, and with that comes attention from venture capitalists. At first, you are flattered by the attention but still have enough funding to play hard to get. Then time passes, and two things happen: First, you develop grand ambitions for new features and team members. Second, you start to run out of money.

Enter the VCs. Now the table has turned, and you find yourself increasingly desperate to impress. It is not uncommon to attend meeting after meeting only to receive the *it's not you, it's me* of the funding world: "We're really excited about your business, but we want to see a few things play out first." And everything I just said applies equally to banks. Plato might also have said, "Banks only lend to the businesses that don't need it."

Instead of spending your most valuable resource—time—chasing down investment, you are better off focusing your energy on gaining traction and building a sustainable revenue stream. Staying lean and maintaining your independence for as long as you can provide you the ability to be flexible and to find the right value proposition for your business.

DON'T FOLLOW THE HERD

The most important lesson we've learned is that you should never be afraid to question the prevailing wisdom. When we first started out, everyone told us that we had to market directly to accountants if we wanted to have a snowball's chance in hell of reaching small businesses. The problem was that many accountants viewed our product as a threat rather than an opportunity. As a result, we found ourselves having to defend our product to our target market.

Instead of fighting an uphill battle or modifying our product to serve that segment, we simply identified a new channel for marketing our product—financial institutions. Our new partners quickly recognized our product as a welcome engagement tool for connecting with and better serving their small-business customers, not a threat. What felt like a risky and perhaps counterintuitive decision at the time turned out to be the best move we could have made.

FINDING BALANCE

LEARNING THE VALUE OF EMOTIONAL INTELLIGENCE

When I was younger, I held the false belief that academic education was the great differentiator when it came to determining success. I believed that the most traditionally intelligent person always came out ahead in life.

As a result, I always found myself in a state of never-ending competition, striving to prove myself among a more academically gifted group of friends and acquaintances.

As I've grown, however, I've come to realize that emotional intelligence is more important when it comes to determining long-term success. I define emotional intelligence as the intrinsic ability for self-awareness, introspection, and motivation.

These abilities, however, aren't learned as easily or as formally as one would learn calculus or computer science. Instead, they're learned from trial and error, observation, and the guidance of other emotionally intelligent individuals.

While I'm far from having mastered these skills, I am at a point in my life where I understand their importance and recognize them in other people. Looking back, I've come to realize that it was my mother who instilled this appreciation of the qualitative aspects of life in me from an early age.

It's OK to Strive for Something Greater

My mother had a comfortable upbringing in a loving middle-class family, but she always had the ambition to strive for something greater. This ambition, however, took an interesting form. Rather than simply seeking social mobility and affluence, my mother instead embraced a broader sense of ambition.

She was uncomfortable with the idea of complacency and looked to improve and grow in everything that she did. She was never satisfied with life as it was and passed down the undying notion that there was something more waiting just around the corner.

I vividly recall a moment from my childhood when I was upset because I wasn't one of the smartest kids in my class. While it may have been a bit melodramatic of an eight-year-old boy, I felt as though I was destined to live my days in the middle of the pack, surpassed by those who seemingly possessed a greater natural academic ability.

My mother caught on to my preteen angst and told me (in no uncertain terms) that I was the only person who could determine my station in life. Natural ability was only one small part of the equation. Instead, it was the burning desire to achieve something greater than a life of quiet desperation that would give me the strength to push forward.

I realized at that moment that ambition was more important than natural ability. She made it clear that it was OK for me to strive for something greater—that ambition was a gift in and of itself.

IF A JOB IS WORTH DOING, IT'S WORTH DOING EXCEPTIONALLY WELL

I've often jokingly compared my mother to Martha Stewart, due in no small part to my mother's perfectionism and boundless attention to detail. Whether she's planning a party, volunteering for some cause, or helping her child with a school project, she puts her full effort into the task at hand. There's a pulsing energy in her actions that leads to amazing results. As a teenager, it drove me crazy—there was no such thing as a lazy day in her house. However, as I've grown, I've found that she was right: if a job is worth doing, it's worth doing exceptionally well.

This inherited mentality has led me to where I am today. Nearly ten years ago, I was working as a consultant doing valuation and M&A work for small and midmarket companies. I was dreadfully unhappy in the role and desperately wanted to make a change. Out of the blue, I was contacted by a corporate recruiter looking for someone to join the strategy team of a Fortune 500 company. I felt that I was unqualified for the role, but I decided to go ahead and apply. After a few interviews, the hiring manager asked me to create a white paper outlining potential alternative uses for the company's assets.

I saw this white paper as the opportunity to prove to myself and to the world that I was qualified for the position, and I threw myself into the project. I created a comprehensive report; when I was done, I had it professionally formatted and bound. During my final interview, I distributed the bound copies of the white paper to the team, who were impressed with the effort.

After being offered the job, I came to find out that the other candidates, who were seemingly better qualified, had put in minimal effort and that it was my over-the-top effort on the white paper that had sealed the deal. That hiring manager was Matt Ankrum, the man who became my cofounder at BodeTree and helped me achieve my dreams of starting my company.

My mother has always been my advocate, confidant, and motivator, and there isn't a single day when I'm not grateful for her influence and stunning emotional intelligence. The lessons she taught me are some of the most valuable I've ever learned, and I believe they're directly responsible for any successes I've achieved in my life.

She taught me the value of emotional intelligence—that it is OK to strive for something greater and that ambition is more important than natural ability. That lesson gave me the confidence and the drive to push myself further than I ever thought I could go. Perhaps more important, my mother taught me that if a job is worth doing, it's worth doing exceptionally well. Throwing yourself into a task and going above and beyond leads to amazing results and opens up unexpected opportunities that just might change your life.

TAKE A ROAD TRIP

I'm a frequent traveler, but more often than not that means hustling from one major airport to the next. My longest travel time usually clocks in at less than five hours. Recently, however, I decided to shake things up and make the fourteen-hour drive from Denver to Phoenix.

I haven't taken a road trip like that since I was a kid, and the experience was fascinating. The process of driving through America for two days led to many realizations about the nature of entrepreneurship and the market I serve. The process was so valuable, in fact, that I think every entrepreneur who finds him- or herself operating in a bubble, especially those on the coasts, should take a road trip and reconnect with the rest of America.

HUMANIZE YOUR UNDERSTANDING OF THE MARKET

When you're an entrepreneur, it is natural to think of your addressable market in terms of statistics. At BodeTree, I've always thought about our market as comprising thirty million small businesses, 90 percent of which don't have organized accounting. It's deceptively easy to do back-of-the-napkin calculations and back into PowerPoint-ready ideas of market penetration.

The reality, however, is far more complicated. I stopped at a number of small businesses on my trip and observed their owners as they worked. It became abundantly clear that every small-business owner is unique, with different motivations, goals, and expectations. While I had an intrinsic understanding of this after working in the industry for years, the process of witnessing small-business owners in action drove the point home with newfound clarity.

This fundamentally human observation of the market my company tries to serve resonated with me on a personal level. I walked away from the experience with a more holistic understanding of the market and my company's ability to serve it.

GAIN A FRESH PERSPECTIVE

When you're building any kind of innovative product, you tend to spend a disproportionate amount of time catering to early adopters. More often than not, these early advocates are young, urban, and relatively sophisticated. When you couple this with the fact that many entrepreneurs base their operations in urban environments where these types congregate, it becomes easy to see how a perception bubble can develop.

I sometimes forget just how big and diverse the United States really is. While driving through small towns and vast stretches of open land, I realized just how insulated my life is from the reality of the individuals I'm trying to serve.

Driving through rural America gave me a fresh understanding of and appreciation for our diverse domestic cultures. Any entrepreneur looking to serve the broad market would be wise to cultivate the same appreciation inside of his or her own business.

BETTER UNDERSTAND THE CHALLENGES OF SCALING YOUR BUSINESS

Perhaps the most significant feeling I experienced on my journey was a feeling of dread regarding the challenge of scaling BodeTree in rural areas. Much of the infrastructure that we take for granted, from high-speed Internet to ubiquitous cell-tower coverage, doesn't exist in the same capacity throughout much of the country.

In essence, the experience helped me broaden my understanding of the market and my company's place in it. Many of my assumptions, such as the general level of technological savvy or quality of infrastructure, were turned on their head once I reached some of the more rural communities along the way.

My understanding of the small-business market evolved and grew more nuanced, and I better recognized the dangers of an insulated urban perspective. Entrepreneurs of all walks can benefit from this type of wake-up call. So if you're looking to reconnect and expand your understanding of the US market, take a road trip this year. You'll definitely learn a thing or two along the way.

HOW TO AVOID ENTREPRENEURIAL BURNOUT

Entrepreneurship is a long and often treacherous journey, and it's easy to encounter periods of burnout along the way. According to the Mayo Clinic, job burnout is defined as "a special type of job stress—a state of physical, emotional, or mental exhaustion combined with doubts about your competence and the value of your work."

If that sounds familiar, you're not alone. Almost everyone experiences burnout at one point or another over the course of his or her career, but entrepreneurs are particularly susceptible. The burden of creating a company from scratch and leading a team builds up over time and can manifest itself in unfortunate ways.

I've dealt with burnout at several different points in the past and know how hard it can be to overcome once it sets in. Fortunately, necessity is the mother of invention. In my desperation to stave off burnout before it causes real problems, I've managed to find a few ways to identify its symptoms and avoid its effects.

CHANGE THE SCENERY

I strongly believe that place has a tremendous effect on both the quality of work you produce and your overall morale. Working from the same place, with the same view, during the same hours reinforces a sense of monotony and can lead to burnout.

Our offices at BodeTree are fun, open, and creative, all things considered. Still, I find myself falling into similar routines and thought patterns when I work from my desk day in and day out. This mental rut of sorts is always a key indicator that feelings of burnout are right around the corner.

When I feel that beginning to take hold, I make an effort to get a change of scenery. Sometimes this means simply getting up and working from a different place in the office. Other times, I'll leave altogether and work from a coffee shop or café. The change of scenery almost always encourages new thoughts and ideas, preventing you from falling into the mental rut that leads to burnout.

EXPLORE YOUR CREATIVE SIDE

Running a business can be stressful, terrifying, and lonely. Even for individuals who have great support networks and cofounders, it can still be difficult to find an outlet to vent. After all, spouses can get concerned about the how your challenges will affect their lives, and fellow entrepreneurs are often too wrapped up in their own difficulties to listen to yours. When you bottle these emotions up, they can easily result in feelings of burnout. Writing, however, is the perfect outlet for explaining, exploring, and digesting everything that you face as an entrepreneur in a healthy way.

Writing is my preferred outlet for creative expression, but any creative outlet will work. The important thing is to find a way to identify and address the feelings that lead to burnout. When you manage the causes of burnout in a healthy, creative way, you rob them of their power over you.

BE IN THE MOMENT

When things start to pile up and feelings of burnout set in, don't panic. Remember to stop and be mindful of the present moment. More often than not, the feelings you're experiencing are related to what you think might happen in the future, not what you're dealing with in the present. Practicing mindfulness and focusing on the current moment can give you a reprieve from the thoughts and concerns that lead to burnout.

The benefits of mindfulness have been well documented, and one *Harvard Business Review* article points out that it takes as little as six seconds of mindful meditation for these benefits to manifest themselves. Quieting your mind and moving away from endless "what-if" scenarios help center you in the present and prepare you to deal with the tasks that lie ahead more effectively.

The key to managing burnout and avoiding its worst effects is to spot its early symptoms and take decisive action before they take hold. Simple things like changing the location of where you choose to work, writing, or being mindful of the present can make all the difference in the world.

FIND THE JOY

There are countless things that keep business founders and leaders awake at night. Clients, employees, investors, and everything in between can, and often do, cause terrible stress and anxiety. The unconscious negativity that results from prolonged and persistent anxiety almost always has seriously detrimental effects on your team, relationships, and personal well-being. The good news is that it doesn't have to be this way. Everyone has the potential to choose a different path—a path of positivity and joy even in the face of the most difficult situations.

This topic comes up frequently at BodeTree, especially when we're raising funds. Fundraising, no matter how well your business is doing, is always a stressful process.

It's the job of potential investors to challenge every assumption and question the very premise of the thing you have worked so hard to create. The juggling act of executing on the opportunities we have in front of us while simultaneously completing a new capital raise will undoubtedly cause stress and anxiety. That's why I've used this calm before the storm to make the case for unrelenting positivity to the team.

It Starts with Self-Awareness

A strong sense of self-awareness is a vital trait that every member of the team needs to develop and nurture. Without it, it's impossible to control your reactions to the trials and tribulations that life so often presents. This is especially important for leaders, as their actions (either conscious or unconscious) set the tone for the entire organization.

The first step toward self-awareness is to recognize and be open about the things that cause stress, anxiety, and negativity in your life. This enables you to prepare yourself and your team for challenging situations well ahead of time. Positivity and negativity are a choice; the only trick is that you have to be self-aware enough to recognize it.

Control Is an Illusion

Humans have a persistent and particularly nasty tendency to try to control everything around them. A strong argument can be made that fruitless attempts at control are generally at the root of all suffering. Business leaders, in particular, tend to box themselves and their team into painful situations when they try to exert control over things that cannot be controlled. This futility leads to anger, frustration, and irrational decisions. Once this behavior takes hold, it builds on itself and can spread like wildfire throughout an organization.

The key to fostering positivity and a functional team is to recognize that control is simply an illusion. Once you stop trying to control your circumstances, you open yourself up to countless possibilities. Understanding this allows you to find new and positive ways to react to the challenges you encounter along your way. The only thing you have control over is your outlook.

FIND THE JOY IN ALL THINGS

Everyone has the ability to find the joy in any circumstance, regardless of how challenging it seems. Joy can often be found in the suffering itself, as it helps you learn more about yourself and grow stronger. It's a choice we have the ability to make. Every situation can be viewed in a positive light if you look from the right angle. I challenge my team to stop and find the good in every situation they encounter. With enough practice, positivity becomes your default setting.

Fostering a spirit of unrelenting positivity, both personally and professionally, doesn't mean that you have to be naive. It is always in everyone's best interest to be in tune with reality and aware of all possible outcomes. The important thing is not to become so caught up in the bad that you lose yourself to anxiety, frustration, and negativity.

It is our choice to be happy and positive in the face of challenges. Positivity and joy are contagious and can quickly shape the very fabric of your reality. As we move forward into the next exciting phase of our business, there will no doubt be challenges. However, I have every confidence that my team will find the joy in every situation and move forward in a spirit of unrelenting positivity.

Leadership Lessons

How I Evolved from Founder to CEO

The act of starting a business and building something from nothing is an intensely personal experience. For most entrepreneurs, there is virtually no separation between business and personal life. As I've mentioned, work is life, and life is work. However, as a business matures, founders must mature alongside it to be successful. Often this means relinquishing the total control to which they have become accustomed.

The very idea of relinquishing control can be a difficult thing for founders to accept. After all, it is often their hard work and attention to detail that brought the business to that point in the first place. However, the behaviors and practices that worked at the early stage of a business rarely translate once a business has reached a point of maturity. That is why so many founders are replaced as CEO once institutional investors join the board.

Over the past few years, I've managed to evolve from being a cofounder/CEO to a true chief executive officer. I've learned that the title of CEO isn't one that you simply bestow on yourself. Rather, it's earned by the way you interact with your team, investors, and board. Here are the three major tasks that I believe founders must accomplish if they want to evolve into a true CEO.

Let Go, and Trust Your Team

The personal connection between an entrepreneur and his or her business can be a great strength early on, but as the business matures, it can transform into a major weakness. At some point, the organization becomes too much for one person to manage, and team members have to take over.

For founders, there is always a huge temptation to sit in on every sales call, review every piece of copy, and test every single software feature that the company develops. Successful CEOs, however, focus on building up the members of their team rather than trying to do their work for them.

Founders look at team members as extra hands, unfortunate necessities that are there simply to execute against their vision. CEOs, on the other hand, look at team members as assets who must be nurtured, developed, and set free. You know you're transitioning from founder to CEO when you stop focusing on the work product people produce and start focusing on the people themselves.

EMBRACE ACCOUNTABILITY

When you're a founder, you're accountable to virtually no one. That reality always makes me think back to the television series *The Office*, in which the buffoonish manager Michael Scott remarks, "Truth be told, I think I thrive under a lack of accountability."

Lack of accountability is both seductive and addictive. The only constraint that a founder knows is one of capital—and good founders can always raise more money. True CEOs, however, know that accountability is a good thing that can help drive the business forward. That's why they create and nurture boards.

I'm currently in the process of forming BodeTree's board of directors. I've found that it is a task that is not to be taken lightly. Finding the right balance of people who add tangible value, who provide insight, and who can hold you accountable is extremely difficult. However, I know that it is the right move. I want to put these constraints on myself and ensure that I'm clearly accountable to my team, investors, and board.

BECOME A SERVANT LEADER

Too many founders look at their business purely in economic terms, especially if they've invested a lot of their personal capital. Leadership and investment, however, are two starkly different things. Founders with the investor mentality look to capitalize on efficiencies and cash out. This leads to harsh and dictatorial leadership styles where the primary goal is personal enrichment.

True CEOs, however, realize how damaging and ineffective that approach can be. Instead, they strive to deliver economic and social benefits through servant leadership. Servant leadership inverts the typical evolutionary concepts of power, whereby one individual at the top of the heap exerts control over those below them. In contrast, the servant leader shares power and aims to make those around him- or herself successful and happy.

In doing so, servant leaders develop true loyalty and support from those they lead and find long-term success. This is not a new concept, yet it is put into practice far less frequently than it deserves. It was Lao-Tzu who wrote, "The highest type of ruler is one of whose existence the people are barely aware. Next comes one whom they love and praise. Next comes one whom they fear. Next comes one whom they despise and defy."

When you compare and contrast the role of a founder with the role of a CEO, it is easy to see why many founders fail to make the jump. Smart investors know the challenges and will push to bring in seasoned CEOs who know how to trust and nurture a team, accept accountability, and practice servant leadership. Founders looking to remain in charge of the business they create should take note—and work to adopt those same traits.

NEVER IGNORE CULTURE

I've made my fair share of mistakes as a leader, but the worst mistake by far was allowing negativity to take root inside my organization. Negativity is like a cancer inside of your company; it grows undetected until suddenly it consumes you. More often than not, bad attitudes start out fairly innocently. Sometimes they can be as simple as a disagreement over a particular strategy. Other times, they can start out as a personality conflict between team members.

Regardless of its origins, unchecked negativity tends to snowball into something that can be fatal for a team. Looking back, I realize that I noticed early signs of this happening in my team but chose to ignore them because I genuinely wanted to think the best of people. Unfortunately, I learned that my inaction allowed the problem to fester and ultimately cause more damage than it should have. Here's how I went wrong.

I DIDN'T HEED MY OWN ADVICE

I firmly believe that at the core of every successful business is an amazing team. Building that team is often one the most difficult and risky challenges you can face as a leader. That's why I've adopted a simple rule that guides all our hiring decisions: we look for people we trust, respect, and admire. It sounds trite, but I've found that if the candidate fits those criteria, everything from cultural fit to skills naturally falls in line. The problem is that I don't always heed my own advice.

It all began when I allowed my lack of patience to get the better of me. We were preparing for a surge in activity, and I grew frustrated while trying to fill a key role that we desperately needed. After going through countless résumés and enduring several excruciatingly bad interviews, I jumped at the first candidate who made a good impression. I didn't take the necessary time to get to know the person and determine whether that person was someone I could truly trust, respect, and admire. Instead, I took the shortsighted, easy way out and set the stage for future problems.

I IGNORED THE CONTAGION

Several months later, my executive team and I started to notice a change in the attitude of some of our team members. We were going through a significant organizational shift at the time, directing our focus toward institutional sales and away from the direct-to-consumer model that we had built up over the course of the past few years.

Unfortunately, not everyone was on board with this shift, and I did not do a good enough job of selling every member of the organization on the vision. The key team member whom I had hired a few months earlier took particular exception to the shift in strategy. I took the traditional steps to offer coaching to shine a light on the issues we were experiencing, but I failed to grasp how contagious an attitude could be.

Instead of recognizing the severity of the situation, I treated it as an isolated incident and moved on. I wanted everyone on my team to be successful and went to great lengths to make excuses for their shortcomings. It was only later on that I realized that I wasn't doing them any favors. Psychological momentum is a powerful force, for better or worse. By not calling out bad behavior, I allowed it to gain momentum and influence others.

Before I knew it, great employees of whom I thought very highly were being drawn into the same downward spiral. Negativity had taken root in that particular team, and I knew then that if I didn't take decisive action, one bad apple would spoil the bunch.

FINALLY, I ELIMINATED THE PROBLEM AT ITS SOURCE

Once I fully realized the severity of the situation and the role I had played in allowing it to happen, I took decisive action. I had to eliminate the source of the problem and stop the rise of negativity in the rest of the team. It required a delicate balance of providing transparency into what was happening while still being respectful of individual privacy. I didn't want to demonize any particular individual, but at the same time I needed the team members to understand what behaviors were considered unacceptable.

My management team and I moved quickly, providing additional clarity about the situation and recognizing our shortcomings. When all was said and done, the rest of the team was fully on board with the direction we were taking, and the negativity disappeared.

This was a difficult time for me as a leader, because I saw all too clearly how my personal failings had allowed the situation to progress out of hand. Still, the lessons I took away from the experience have proved to be invaluable. Negativity simply cannot be tolerated in any organization. This does not mean that dissenting voices should be ignored. To the contrary, disagreements should be heard and thoughtfully considered.

However, once a decision has been made, the entire organization needs to rally around it. If any team member continues to spread negativity and dissent, his or her attitude will act like a cancer inside your organization. As a leader, you have to make sure that you avoid this situation by hiring people whom you trust, respect, and admire. Then, if you see the early signs of contagious negativity, you have to eliminate it at the source. The process might be painful, but your organization will be the healthier for it.

TRANSPARENCY IS A BEHAVIOR, NOT A BUZZWORD

In business, leaders often throw around terms like *transparency* and *clarity* casually and without consequence, as if merely paying lip service to such concepts is sufficient to convince customers and employees alike. In reality, very few leaders practice true transparency within their organizations, and even fewer do it with their customers.

Clear and transparent communication are not simple skills that can be adopted and then dropped at the first sign of trouble but rather must be practiced in thought, word, and deed. Without a culture of transparency, organizations quickly come unglued, and little bumps—like an angry client or misinformed employee—turn into mountains. But with busy schedules, seemingly endless task lists, and diverse clients and personnel, creating a smooth flow of communication can be a challenge.

No one is perfect when it comes to transparent leadership, and I've had my share of shortcomings in my role as CEO. The key lesson I've learned is that transparency is a habit—and like any habit, it takes constant reinforcement.

THROW OUT THE CONFUSING LANGUAGE

Back in high school, I had the choice of studying one of three languages: French, Spanish, or Latin. Thinking that the Latin class would be small and therefore easy, I opted for it. This decision, as with many best-laid teenage plans, proved to be a mistake. Not only was the subject matter wildly confusing, the class was taught by a semiretired Austrian man who had absolutely no patience for anyone under the age of fifty. In short, it was a difficult situation that left me with a distaste for all things Latin.

Now the only time I encounter Latin is in legal documents, where it is used for the explicit purpose of obfuscating the writer's meaning. Lawyers aren't the only ones guilty of this, of course—intentionally confusing jargon can be found across a number of industries, including both accounting and banking. Many professionals try to keep things intentionally confusing so that they're needed to translate. It's a perverse form of job security, I suppose, and one that has always rubbed me the wrong way.

I've always lived by the old Mark Twain quote: "Never use a five-dollar word when a fifty-cent word will do." The idea that ideas can be clear, clean, and simple is something that sits at the very core of my leadership strategy and everything we do at BodeTree. There's no need for confusing, intentionally opaque language, whether it's internal to your company or customer facing. Commit to clear, straightforward language, and a culture of transparency will follow.

REMEMBER THE VALUE OF STORYTELLING

It isn't enough to list out facts and directives for teams or clients. In order for people to understand, you have to tell a compelling story. Not every communication has to be a novel, but putting your company's mission, strategy, and operational directives into a coherent narrative helps you, your team members, and your customers better comprehend and remember key points.

Here's the secret about clarity: it takes work to achieve. There is no magic formula for ensuring that people are aligned and that they share a common understanding of the mission or task. The only way to succeed is for all team members, regardless of rank or position, to make sure that clarity comes first in all interactions.

WHY BULLIES MAKE BAD LEADERS

There is a dangerous and destructive idea fomenting in American society today, and it permeates almost every aspect of modern life. From politics to business, our society is increasingly mistaking aggression for strength and bullying for leadership. One need only look at the nature of Donald Trump's bombastic, aggressive, and wildly popular presidential campaign for proof of this disturbing trend. In times of difficulty, the allure of the bully is seductive yet ultimately disappointing. Bullies might be good at gaining power, but they make terrible leaders.

My experience in leadership is limited to the world of business. I've never led men into battle or won an election. However, I believe that the core principles of good leadership transcend boundaries and definition. It's up to leaders and followers alike to recognize bullies when they rear their ugly heads and instead put their faith in those who lead by strength, sincerity, and example.

NEVER MISTAKE AGGRESSION FOR STRENGTH

So why do we think that bullies make for good leaders? The blame lies in our evolutionary history. Throughout our time on this earth, the loudest, most aggressive member of the group became leader. As a result, our brains have evolved to associate aggression with high status. That's why even normally rational people often sympathize with Trump despite the fact that his proclamations are frequently nonsensical.

I think that the real problem here is that people mistake aggression for strength. In reality, strength of character has virtually nothing to do with aggression. We as a species simply fall victim to our evolutionary biases. Real strength comes from a quiet determination to do what is right, make the difficult decisions, and serve the interests of the team. In my personal experience, the individuals who make the best leaders aren't aggressive. Instead, their quiet confidence speaks louder than any blustering.

RECOGNIZE THE STRENGTH IN HUMILITY

If you think about the demagogues and bullies we see throughout society, you'll quickly realize that they have one thing in common: pride. Indeed, arrogance and pride together are the hallmark of the bully, and they fundamentally undermine the ability to lead. Instead, I believe that effective leaders are humble in thought, word, and deeds.

BE A SERVANT LEADER

As I mentioned earlier, the servant leader stands in stark contrast to the bully by sharing power and focusing his or her attention on making those around him- or herself successful and happy.

It's time that we as a people fought back against our primal urges and learned to better reject bullies. Instead, we must look to servant leaders who can be successful in the long term. Whether it's in business or politics, servant leaders succeed where bullies fail.

MANAGING ANXIETY AND DEPRESSION

AN ENTREPRENEUR'S GUIDE TO MANAGING ANXIETY

Building and running a business is often a difficult, stressful, and uncertain process. In a day and age in which we idolize successful entrepreneurs, we are encouraged to buy into the false narrative of the "rugged individualist," a person who is simultaneously unflappable and confident. In reality, however, this narrative couldn't be further from the truth.

Almost every week, I hear from entrepreneurs who are overstressed and who are dealing with anxiety. I've cherished the opportunity to talk to these individuals and offer my support. I've learned a lot about managing stressful situations while building BodeTree, and I remind everyone that even the most iconic entrepreneurs have struggled with uncertainty, depression, and anxiety at different points along their journeys. Entrepreneurs shouldn't be ashamed to admit their own struggles. If you find yourself struggling with anxiety, don't despair. There are ways to overcome these challenges—no matter how large they may seem.

BE OPEN ABOUT YOUR CHALLENGES

If you find yourself struggling with anxiety, it's important to stop and seek out a fresh perspective before you fall into a negative spiral. Life, like business, is a journey full of ups and downs. Those ups and downs always seem more extreme to the people experiencing them firsthand than they do to those on the outside. If you find yourself in a difficult position and feel as if the walls are closing in on you, reach out to someone with a bit of distance. This person's unbiased assessment of your situation will provide a fresh perspective on things. Chances are that you'll walk away with the realization that things aren't as bad as you thought.

Mentors can be an excellent resource for these types of conversations, but if you find yourself without a trusted mentor, then reach out to other people you trust, respect, and admire. It doesn't matter if it's a friend, spouse, colleague, or family member—the important thing is that you find someone with whom you can be absolutely open no matter what.

USE COGNITIVE BEHAVIORAL THERAPY

Stress and anxiety occur when your mind turns against itself, allowing unhelpful and damaging thoughts and ideas to take hold and wreak havoc. One technique for overcoming such thoughts is cognitive behavioral therapy, or CBT. The core idea behind CBT is that an individual can change behavior, thinking, or emotions by understanding and reorganizing the way those three elements interact with one another.

Thinking about CBT, I'm often reminded of a quote by the stoic philosopher Epictetus, who said, "People are disturbed not by events but by the view they take of them." If you can identify and understand not only what triggers anxiety but also how you respond to it, you can start to deconstruct the situation. Start by identifying your thoughts, emotions, behaviors, and even physical reactions to the stimuli that cause stress.

From there, try to figure out which element you're dealing with at the moment, then work to change the situation. If you're having pervasive unwanted thoughts, recognize them for what they are and don't let them take hold. If you're experiencing a physical reaction such as exhaustion or migraines, don't try to ignore it. If you commit to taking the situation head on, one step at a time, you'll find that it becomes far more manageable.

KEEP EVERYTHING IN PERSPECTIVE

Business Insider recently published a great article about the depression epidemic in the start-up community. According to the article, only 7 percent of the general population reports suffering from depression, but a whopping 30 percent of founders report dealing with its effects, including anxiety. That statistic is staggering, but it's entirely believable. Entrepreneurship is a deeply personal journey, and it's incredibly difficult to separate your individual identity from the business that you're trying to create. Business setbacks (of which there are many) seem like personal setbacks, and anxiety can quickly take root.

The key is to always keep things in perspective. Life, like business, is a journey full of ups and downs. When talking to entrepreneurs who are going through a rough patch, I often encourage them to think back to high school. For most of us, there were moments in our high school lives that seemed to be monumentally important at the time but that in retrospect seem childish.

At the time, of course, the pain and anxiety that you experienced was real and raw. However, the more distance you gain from the situation, the less painful it becomes. While the problems that you're facing right here and right now may seem insurmountable, it's important to realize that these, too, will pass and fade in time.

There will be bumps and setbacks on any entrepreneurial journey, but remember that you're not alone. Find someone to talk to, use cognitive behavioral therapy techniques, and keep things in perspective. No matter how dark a situation looks, it never is as bad as it seems. Remember that almost every entrepreneur has been in the same situation at one time or another. You can and will overcome.

DON'T LOSE YOURSELF TO DEPRESSION

It seems as though every other week I read about another promising young entrepreneur gone too soon. This week, we learned of the early passing of two more promising young entrepreneurs. While I don't claim to know exactly what happened in these particular cases, I do know that the stresses of entrepreneurship can take their toll on people, both physically and emotionally.

Depression is a huge problem among entrepreneurs, and it's time we did something about it. I don't have the answers, but I've learned a few things along my personal entrepreneurial journey that have helped me navigate difficult situations.

LIVE TO FIGHT ANOTHER DAY

Entrepreneurs have to accept that the odds are stacked against their success. Most new business ventures fail, and even those that are eventually successful take a long time to get off the ground. Setbacks will outnumber successes, and there's a good chance that most days will be stressful. That's the game we chose to play, and the ability to embrace these realities is what makes us entrepreneurs.

Still, when challenges pile up, it's easy to feel as if the world is ending and as if we're failures. I recently had lunch with a good friend who was in the process of shuttering his third start-up in seven years. During our conversation, I reminded him that in his brief career so far, he's accomplished more than the vast majority of people do in decades. His pedigree and experience put him in the top 1 percent of people in his age group, and, as a result, his opportunities are vast. Sure, the latest venture didn't work out—but he can, and will, live to fight another day.

Wherever you find yourself at this point in your life, there is a very good chance that your current endeavor will not be your last. In fact, many of the most successful entrepreneurs in the world hit their stride on the second or third attempt. Consider the case of Mark Cuban. Before he struck it big by selling his business to Yahoo, Cuban had a string of failures. After failing as a cook, carpenter, and even a waiter, he remarked,

"I've learned that it doesn't matter how many times you failed. You only have to be right once. I tried to sell powdered milk. I was an idiot lots of times, and I learned from them all."

The lesson here is that there are second (and third and fourth) acts in life, and it's important to remember that whenever you encounter failure.

DON'T BE AFRAID TO GET HELP

I'm fortunate to have a fantastic support network I can call on when I need help. My family members and friends are always there when I need them, whether to listen to my struggles or to lend a hand. Not everyone is as lucky.

Entrepreneurs need to be able to reach out for help when they need it. This can be difficult in a world where everyone feels the need to be "crushing it" all the time. Asking for help can be seen as a sign of weakness, which leads to people simply keeping their difficulties to themselves.

We in the entrepreneur community need to change this mentality. People should feel free to get help without the fear of judgment, and it's going to take a few brave influencers to initiate the change. I know a few people in the industry who care about this deeply, including Structure Capital (a team of high-profile venture investors based out of San Francisco), but more are needed. There are good people out there who want to help. It's just a matter of having the courage to reach out.

There will be bumps and setbacks on any entrepreneurial journey, but remember that you're not alone. Keep your challenges in perspective and live to fight another day. No matter how dark a situation looks, it never is as bad as it seems. Most important, don't be afraid to get help.

How I Learned to Deal with Uncertainty

The only thing that is certain in life is uncertainty. There are countless things that keep business founders and leaders awake at night. Clients, employees, investors, and everything in between can, and often does, cause terrible uncertainty—and, along with it, stress and anxiety. We all deal with uncertainty in different ways, but coping with it healthfully is something few very few manage to do.

I've been guilty of allowing uncertainty to get to me in the context of running BodeTree. It's a very exciting time for us, as we grow rapidly and work with new partners every day. We're also about to begin our latest fundraising round to add some fuel to our growth engine.

Fundraising, no matter how well your business is doing, is always a stressful process. When you combine a capital raise with dramatic growth and the possibility of several game-changing partnerships coming online, it's safe to say that you're operating in an uncertain environment.

I was lamenting my situation with one of my trusted mentors the other day, and, as usual, he provided sage advice. He said, "Chris, you have to understand that maturity of mind is the capacity to endure uncertainty." His simple but profound words struck a chord with me. Uncertainty is part of life, but it doesn't have to be an anxiety-inducing, momentum-sapping experience. Instead, he helped me realize that everyone has the potential to choose a different path—a path of positivity and joy even in the face of the most uncertain situations.

A Mature Mind Is Self-Aware

A strong sense of self-awareness is a vital trait that every member of the team needs to develop and nurture. Without it, it's impossible to control your reaction to the trials and tribulations that life so often presents. This is especially important for leaders, as their actions (either conscious or unconscious) set the tone for the entire organization.

The first step toward self-awareness is to recognize and be open about the things that cause stress, anxiety, and negativity in your life. This enables you to prepare yourself and your team for challenging situations well ahead of time. Positivity and negativity are a choice; the only trick is that you have to be self-aware enough to recognize it.

A MATURE MIND RECOGNIZES THAT CONTROL IS AN ILLUSION

Humans have a persistent and particularly nasty tendency to try to control everything around them. A strong argument can be made that fruitless attempts at control are generally at the root of all suffering. Business leaders, in particular, tend to box themselves and their team into painful situations when they try to exert control over things that cannot be controlled. This futility leads to anger, frustration, and irrational decisions. Once this behavior takes hold, it builds on itself and can spread like wildfire throughout an organization.

The key to fostering positivity and a functional team is the ability to recognize that control is simply an illusion. Once you stop trying to control your circumstances, you open yourself up to countless possibilities. Understanding this allows you to find new and positive ways to react to the challenges you encounter along the way. The only thing you have control over is your outlook.

A MATURE MIND HAS THE ABILITY TO FIND THE JOY IN ANY SITUATION

Everyone has the ability to find the joy in any circumstance, regardless of how challenging it seems. Joy can often be found in the suffering itself, as it helps you learn more about yourself and grow stronger. It's a choice we have the ability to make. Almost every situation can be viewed in a positive light if you look at it from the right angle. I challenge my team members to pause and find the good in every situation they encounter. With enough practice, positivity becomes your default setting.

Fostering a spirit of unrelenting positivity in the face of uncertainty, both personally and professionally, doesn't mean that you have to be naive. It is always in everyone's best interest to be in tune with reality and aware of all possible outcomes. The important thing is not to become so caught up in the bad that you lose yourself to anxiety, frustration, and negativity.

It is our choice to be happy and positive in the face of uncertainty. Positivity and joy are contagious and can quickly shape the very fabric of your reality. As we move forward into the next exciting phase of our business, I don't doubt that we will encounter challenges and uncertain situations. However, I have every confidence that my team and I will be prepared to find the joy in every situation and move forward in a spirit of unrelenting positivity.

MANAGING THE STRESS OF BEING AN ENTREPRENEUR

It's clichéd to say that entrepreneurs wear many hats, but there's no escaping truth. Entrepreneurs and business leaders have to balance the needs of business strategy and business execution alongside family and their personal needs. With so many aspects of life demanding equal attention, it's easy to become overwhelmed.

I know this feeling all too well—at the moment, I'm dealing with a sick family, a fundraising round, a busy writing and television schedule, and a hellish travel agenda, not to mention the daily work of running a growing company. You could safely say that I'm feeling a bit overwhelmed at the moment.

Fortunately, I have plenty of experience coping with the feelings of being overwhelmed by the responsibilities of my life. Over the years, I've learned three coping mechanisms that enable me to not only deal with feelings of being overwhelmed but also thrive.

BE IN THE MOMENT

When things start to pile up and you start to feel overwhelmed by the tasks ahead, don't panic. Remember to stop and be mindful of the present moment. More often than not, the anxiety and stress that entrepreneurs experience is due to what they think might happen in the future, not what they're dealing with in the present. Practicing mindfulness and focusing on the current moment can give you a reprieve from the thoughts and concerns that cause anxiety.

The benefits of mindfulness have been well documented, and a recent *Harvard Business Review* article points out that it takes as little as six seconds of mindful meditation for these benefits to manifest themselves. Quieting your mind and moving away from the endless "what-if" scenarios helps center you in the present and prepares you to deal more effectively with the tasks that lie ahead.

PICK YOUR PRIORITIES

No matter how talented or motivated you are, it's impossible to do everything at once, so stop trying. The best way to dig out of an overwhelming situation is to pick your top priorities and work from there. Prioritization is difficult for many entrepreneurs, because everything seems to be equally important at first glance. When we step back and practice mindfulness, however, we realize that this isn't the case. It's always possible to prioritize things in your life; it just isn't always easy.

I think nearly everyone has heard some variation of the "glass and rubber balls" quote, but here's the short version for those who haven't. In life, we're forced to juggle, and some of the balls are made of glass and shatter when dropped, while others are made of rubber and always bounce back.

When juggling priorities, it's important to remember that matters of the heart, be they relationships, family, or personal fulfillment, are made of glass. If you drop them, they're irreparably damaged. Work, on the other hand, is rubber. Even when you make a terrible mistake and drop the ball, it always bounces back. The key to happiness is recognizing which ball is which.

For me, priorities are absolute and fall into three categories. My first priorities are the needs of family. That ball is made of glass, and I do my best to protect it. My second priority is my company. For entrepreneurs and leaders, work needs to be a higher priority than it is for most people. The reason for this is that it isn't just about dealing with your job. As the leader of a company, you have many people who depend on you, including team members, clients, and investors. The third priority is personal fulfillment. If you've taken care of your family and your team, then you have the right to focus on yourself. Clearly defining these priorities makes dealing with even the most overwhelming of situations more manageable.

ACCEPT IMPERFECTION

Last but not least, it's important to learn to accept imperfection. Perfection is an unattainable goal, and anyone who thinks otherwise is deluded. It's far better to recognize that we live in an imperfect world and that sometimes our best is good enough.

This applies to both work and personal life. Sometimes it's better to let the housework slide so that you can play with your kid—or to relinquish control on a project rather than micromanage it. Learning to accept imperfection enables you to keep moving forward, and that's precisely what you need to do when you're feeling overwhelmed.

Everyone gets overwhelmed from time to time, but it doesn't need to lead to anxiety or excessive stress. The trick is to make sure that you stay in the moment, pick your priorities, and accept imperfection. Once you do those three simple things, you'll find yourself in a good position from which to overcome the challenges you face so that you can move forward with confidence.

Don't Be Afraid to Seek Support

After writing about anxiety and depression for *Forbes*, I heard from dozens of entrepreneurs who were suffering but who felt that they had no place else to turn. I did my best to connect with everyone who reached out to me over the phone and listen to his or her story. More often than not, I found myself giving very similar advice to the people I spoke to despite their diverse backgrounds. It seems simple, but sometimes simple answers offer the best solutions to complex problems.

Seek Out a Fresh Perspective

If you find yourself struggling with depression or anxiety, it's important to stop and seek out a fresh perspective before you fall into a negative spiral. Life, like business, is a journey full of ups and downs. Those ups and downs always seem more extreme to the people experiencing them firsthand, but often outsiders have a more reasonable view of things.

Recognize What You Can Control and What You Can't

More often than not, anxiety and depression in business have their roots in the illusion of control. We all want to control the world around us, but trying to exert our will on things that cannot be changed is the very definition of futility.

Many of the entrepreneurs I speak to spend an inordinate amount of time and effort attempting to control the feelings of their investors, customers, or team members. It's only after they recognize that they have no control over such things that they are able to focus on the elements of their life and business that they *can* influence. Once you let go of futile efforts, you'll feel a tremendous weight lifted, and you'll be ready to move on.

Take Baby Steps

Once you've sorted out what you can control and what you can't, the next step is to create a linear and segmented plan for moving forward. When you take baby steps every single day, you'll create a sense of momentum that will carry you forward. Problems can feel overwhelming, but when you take the time to break them down into bite-size chunks, they suddenly seem a lot less scary and a lot more manageable.

It's my sincere hope that these simple suggestions will help people cope with the challenges they encounter. There will be bumps and setbacks on any entrepreneurial journey, but remember that you're not alone. There are plenty of people who are willing to listen and offer fresh perspectives. They can help you recognize what you can control and what you can't. From there, you can take baby steps to move forward, pulling yourself out of the spiral of anxiety and depression.

As always, if you find yourself without anyone to talk to, feel free to reach out to me at chris@bodetree.com. I'm always happy to connect with fellow entrepreneurs and lend an ear when needed.